becoming
Divinely Human

becoming
Divinely Human

A Direct Path to Embodied Awakening

CC LEIGH

Wolfsong Press
Portland, Oregon

Publisher's Note

This publication is designed to provide accurate and authoritative information in regard to the subject matter covered. It is sold with the understanding that the publisher and author are not hereby providing psychological, financial, legal, or other professional services. If expert assistance or counseling is needed, the services of a competent professional should be sought.

Wolfsong Press
Portland, Oregon
www.divinelyhuman.com
USA

Cover and book design by zoesnyder.com

Printed in the United States of America

ISBN 9780-0-9835462-1-4

Library of Congress Catalog Control Number: 2011932933

For my beloved Michael~
Your love has given me wings.

CONTENTS

INTRODUCTION

A wave of awakening is rising upon the shores of the world right now, a ripeness for change, for a deep understanding of what it means to be *divinely human*. It's due, in part, to an unprecedented convergence of qualities in the world and in human bodies contributing to this rising tide of transformation. For example, many people currently have:

- sufficient wealth (provision for basic needs) so that people have leisure time available to devote to spiritual inquiry;
- sufficient opportunity to have grown tired of chasing after fulfillment through material goods and status;
- sufficient lifespan to mature into readiness for awakening;
- sufficient education and discriminating intelligence for a significant degree of self-knowledge;
- sufficient access to a great diversity of spiritual teachings from around the world, much of which is now translated into English and available at our fingertips through the Internet;
- sufficient understanding of the human psyche to make healing from our psychological wounds and conditioning more possible than in the past;
- and—very importantly—sufficient social tolerance (though not perfect by any means) of religious, intellectual, and spiritual diversity to allow for individual exploration and free thinking.

All of these elements combine to create an unprecedented drive and opportunity for spiritual awakening on a scale than has never existed before.

What do I mean by the term "divinely human"? Divinely human people are those who have awakened to a direct, ongoing experience of their inseparable unity with the ineffable essence—Consciousness—that both *is* and *gives rise to* all that we experience, while paradoxically awakening as their unique human selves, which appear to be separate and distinct from any other form.

Your destiny, if you are drawn to this book, is to discover **all** of who you are and live that as the ground and substance of your life: to become divinely human. This is a profound, life-changing transformation, not just a temporary shift. If you are feeling a strong heart-yearning to awaken, you also have the capacity for that awakening—it is in your genes, it is your birthright. This book describes the key elements that support an *embodied* awakening, which is distinct in many regards from a more transcendental type of awakening.

Embodied awakening is inclusive. It does not pathologize the human ego, personality, or conditioning, and it does not further the split that almost everyone feels at their core, the split between what they consider their "good self" and their "bad self," between their "higher self" and their "ego" or between their "head" and their "heart." It embraces the entire territory of being human, with profound love and compassion for how difficult it is to be here, in life, given the vulnerability of our bodies, minds, and emotions. Embodied awakening is a process of learning to bring our deepest thoughts, feelings, longings, and fears all into the "room" of mutual engagement where they can be transformed by the powerful light of conscious Presence. We awaken in an embodied way when we realize our essence to be infinite, unchanging Consciousness—a Consciousness that not only *witnesses* everything arising in the manifest world, but is also, mysteriously, the very *essence* of everything, including all aspects of what we are. In other words, we realize that there is just Onlyness, and we are That.

How that all happens is what this book is about. Divinely human, embodied awakenings don't necessarily look or sound like typical, idealized descriptions of "enlightenment," and the teachers and other practitioners of this path are not perfected beings in the usual sense. We're works in progress and will remain so as long as we live. Many spiritual teachings focus on an end point so far removed from real lives as to be virtually impossible to attain. This teaching, by contrast, is about something tangible and attainable for many, while also being a profoundly serious process of transformation. Divinely human awakening is so real, satisfying, and compassionate for the challenges inherent in being here that those who experience it say they wouldn't trade it for the world. This awakening brings the end of seeking, typically within a couple of years of active involvement in this Way.

It's my pleasure, my privilege, and my passion to help ordinary people embody this profound awakening, so that they begin to live fulfilled, divinely human lives.

Who "we" are

At the start of each chapter, I offer "Our Story"—a brief summary of what many divinely human people experienced along the way to their full embodied awakenings. "We" refers to the folks—the friends, students, and colleagues—I've had the honor of knowing, whose struggles, illuminations, and courageous hearts have taught me so much more than I could ever have learned in isolation.

The rest of the book is my own version, in my own words, of how I see the awakening process unfolding, both in myself and in others, and does not attempt to speak for anyone else.

Becoming divinely human

Encoded deep in your inherent genetic and energetic code lies the potential for full integrated awakening. In many ways, you have been on this journey for millennia. Generation after generation of people have slowly been developing the capacity for discovering and understanding who and what they are. You have inherited a genetic potential on the physical plane, and have also been evolving on the soul plane through eons to come to this point in time, here and now, when the possibility of many people awakening into their divinely human lives has arrived.

In the past, some individuals broke through the veil of confusion, plumbed the Mystery of existence, and found ways to speak about it. Jesus, the Buddha, Lao Tsu, Mohammed, and many others less famous had direct experience of their inseparable unity with all of creation and the divinity that gives it life. They have tended to be singular beings, born and living in isolation from others who might have awakened in the same generation. Their revelatory teachings were set down by those who followed them, but the teachings typically grew distorted because their followers had not had the same experience. History has shown us the unhappy consequences that can occur when a teaching and its underlying Mystery become conceptualized into a doctrine that people *believe* in, rather than fully *realizing* and *embodying*.

In our present time, not just one or two but many people are undergoing profound personal transformations, and embodying their understanding of the deepest Mystery of human existence. Because we are able to share our experiences with one another in real time, we are able to map the territory of awakening more effectively than ever before. In turn, we're able to help more people awaken in the most direct and auspicious manner possible.

Profound life shifts typically begin with a growth phase, then a period of deconstruction, followed by initiatory shifts and illuminations, and then a time of integrating what has been realized. This book begins with deconstruction—what I call the *darkness before dawn*—when it might feel like your life is falling apart, or you're failing, or maybe you're convinced that nothing will ever bring you the awakening you long for. Does any of this sound familiar? Or perhaps you're having some amazing awakening experiences, but find yourself struggling to bring the rest of your life into alignment with what you're discovering?

My story

That's how it happened for me. My "growth phase" began around 1987, when I started having unusual inner experiences and felt very drawn to undertake spiritual inquiry in earnest. For the next several years, I explored subtle realms with the help of inner (as well as outer) guides. I was an avid learner, and felt quite powerful as I learned techniques to create my life through focus and intention. I even became a teacher of "light body" work.

However, the sense of expanded consciousness I often felt was not sustainable for me. I hit a wall. My life wasn't working out as I expected, and I fell into crippling self-doubt that became broad-scale skepticism about all of the spiritual work I'd been doing. I couldn't tell what was "true" and what was imaginary, and I felt like a fraud. Without any framework to help me understand what was happening, I was adrift. I felt betrayed by my teachers, since they offered no support or assistance for the type of crisis I was experiencing. And I felt abandoned by my inner guides, as well, because I wasn't receiving trustable information. All of my worst fears about myself loomed large and I spiraled down into a very dark place. This was my "darkness before dawn"—but I had no idea there would ever *be* a dawn.

I was unable to continue the type of work I'd been doing. I went into a free-fall that cost me my home and my community, as I moved across country to stay with a friend who took me in. I felt very broken and dysfunctional. I assumed my problems were all my fault. I had no idea that they could be the symptoms of a significant transformation underway.

Life was pretty bleak, but it went on somehow. I borrowed a small RV from my friend, and for several years wandered wherever the wind blew me. During that unstructured time I began doing open-ended meditations, just being quiet and still, curious about what I would discover. I was seeking truth. I distrusted what I had believed in or taken on faith, and became dedicated to finding something more real. I found inspiration and guidance in the written words of Paul Brunton, and also began following the prompts of my innermost Being. Gradually, my inner inquiries became deeper and more profound. By grace (surely not by merit, because I was an ordinary and very flawed person), something opened up to reveal the ground, Source, and substance of All That

Is. As I dissolved into That, losing all personal boundaries and reference points, I knew I had returned to my true *home*.

Yet, as remarkable as it was to merge repeatedly into the Absolute, where all my questions dissolved in that perfect, still womb of Being, *I* always re-emerged at some point. And "I" was still as confused and flawed as ever. There was a big disconnect between my spiritual realization and my human condition. For years I searched for keys to bringing the two together, in spite of being urged by Advaita-oriented friends to disavow my mind, emotions, and reactions. They advised me to hold only to the peace of Consciousness and transcend (ignore) the rest, but I instinctively knew that wasn't the point, or the path—at least not for me.

Gradually, I became more whole and intact. In 1995, I "landed" into what I now call divinely human awakeness: I knew *what* I was (Consciousness), and I relaxed into being *who* I was as the individual person called "CC." At that point, I realized I was no longer seeking.

The process of integrating that awakening continued over the next several years. By chance, I found a copy of Saniel Bonder's newly-published book, *Waking Down*, at a local book sale in Ft. Collins, CO, where I had settled. I was intrigued by the manner in which Saniel was embracing *both* spiritual realization and human individuality. In 1999, I visited Saniel's community in Marin County, California, and by the end of that year, moved there to explore embodied awakening with others who were on the same track. Having spent so much time more or less isolated from other awakening people, it was very exciting to enter a community where such awakenings were happening with a degree of regularity.

Saniel was encouraging his students to practice "mutuality" with one another (as well as with him), and that was new for me. Engaging in relationship this way brought me right up against my dysfunctional patterns, and challenged me to look into—and endorse—myself more fully than I ever had done before. In so doing, I dropped into much greater embodiment than I had known possible.

By late 2001, with Saniel's blessing, I became a teacher of Waking Down in Mutuality. I had known for many years that I was destined to help others awaken, but had not found the right vehicle for doing that until I got involved with Waking Down. So much of what Saniel was teaching was reminiscent of the process I had endured—with the addition of a supportive framework to help people navigate the process much more auspiciously. Being a teacher has given me the opportunity to learn how utterly unique every person is in their awakening process, and to develop effective skills and some new processes to support them along the way. I was, and still am, very happy to offer my support so no one has to suffer to the degree I did in order to awaken and become divinely human.

If you'd like to read more about how the in-depth exploration of conscious embodiment called *Waking Down in Mutuality* began and evolved over the years, please visit **divinelyhuman.com**

About this book

This book encompasses the process of becoming divinely human. It describes the various shifts you will likely encounter, plus a number of understandings and simple practices that will support you in achieving the permanent, unshakeable realization that is your birthright. Such major life transitions can be very confusing, even frightening. This book offers support and guidance to light your way.

However, the program described in this book may go against much of what you've been taught. You may find it counterintuitive. It may sound crazy to you, or too difficult, to lean *into* your places of pain and distress rather than finding ways to fix or avoid feeling them. Yet it is this very willingness to consciously experience what you're feeling that becomes your gateway to landing in your body as your whole, true, and awakened Self. It's not easy, and I'm not trying to sell this as a feel-good, make-your-life-a-bowl-of-cherries program. However, if you find yourself already somewhere in the midst of this mysterious process, this book will help make navigating through it a good deal easier.

In founding Waking Down in Mutuality, Saniel Bonder used many evocative terms and descriptions to articulate the process he and his students were experiencing as they came into embodied awakenings and then began to live their awakenings together in mutuality. I especially acknowledge Saniel for using the term *divinely human* to refer to the type of integrated embodied awakening he was pioneering and teaching. In addition, Saniel deserves full credit for coining or giving unique meanings to many other terms like *core wound, rot, hypermasculine, greenlighting, second birth, embodied feeling-witness consciousness, wakedown shakedown,* and *recognition yoga* that have come into familiar usage within the Waking Down community of practice. These terms will appear occasionally in this book, although I'm not inclined to rely too much on that particular terminology. I prefer to present my understandings in my own words. Those understandings are, however, very informed by my decade of in-depth experience with Waking Down, as a student, then as a teacher, and now as a senior teacher.

The elaborations in each chapter reflect my unique realization and way of seeing, and are not necessarily the way other teachers and mentors in Waking Down would articulate things. The Waking Down community makes room for a variety of expressions, and it is this very mixture of views and insights that makes this work so rich and useful for others who are in the process of coming fully alive and awake.

In addition to the contributions Saniel and other teachers and participants in Waking Down in Mutuality have made to my understanding of embodied awakening, I also want to acknowledge how much I have learned from Ann Weiser Cornell and her Inner Relationship Focusing work (which, in turn, evolved from the seminal work of Eugene Gendlin, who developed the original Focusing process). Inner Relationship Focusing is a highly-refined technology for getting in touch with inner dynamics that typically lie beneath the threshold of awareness, and befriending them from a state of Presence so they can open up and organically evolve. My Inseeing Process™ (Chapter 5), developed for people who are awakening, incorporates many elements of Inner Relationship Focusing as well as understandings inherent in Waking Down and my own life experience.

This book is designed to function as a handbook to help de-mystify awakening and provide you with an overall framework for what happens as you become divinely human. It presents a series of steps that have proven to be very effective for many people. However, since each person's actual awakening will be unique, and not really as linear as presented here, keep in mind that different parts of the book will speak to you at different phases of your process, and will mean more to you as you have your own experiences to reference. Feel free to work with the parts that resonate, and come back to other parts when they are more relevant to your individual process.

A cyclical process

The process itself is more cyclical than linear. Practicing the early steps leads to new insights and initiations, which leads to more available energy (and need) to revisit the earlier steps for deeper work, which in turn leads to greater awakenings, etc. Even after a permanent divinely human awakening has occurred, these cyclical dynamics will continue as your Conscious nature brings more light and spaciousness into the "tight squeeze" places in your human self.

Because each person's dynamic is so unique, you won't find scripted programs here that tell you to do thus-and-such in a disciplined way. Those sorts of formulaic teachings, typically given to large groups wholesale, will not help you now. Still, this book will provide guidance with respect to the inevitable question, "What can I *do*?" that will arise at different times in your personal unfolding.

This book is not meant to replace direct body-to-body contact with people who can help you tailor your own program to your needs of the moment. Individualized attention from teacher-coaches, participation in live events, and support from peers and mentors (and therapists as needed) is an essential part of what makes this work so effective for so many (this is described more fully in Chapter 7: Support). It is hoped that this book will give you some initial understanding of what embodied awakening is all about, and then you can decide if, and how much, you personally wish to engage with the Waking Down community.

A note on capitalization

In general, I capitalize words that refer to the infinite and total Self, the "divine" dimension of what is, to make a distinction when that word can also refer to something that is within the realm of finite experience. For example, Consciousness with a capital "C" refers to its infinite, all-inclusive transcendent aspect, while consciousness with a small "c" refers to ordinary daily awareness. I do not mean to create artificial distinctions between that which is infinite and divine and that which is manifest, but merely to point toward something that might be useful, conceptually, to support apperception of the truth.

A little more on what I mean by "divinely human"

There are so many ways that people think of and relate to the Ultimate Mystery that it is difficult to find any one way to speak about it without being off-putting to some, or leaving others out. As people evolve spiritually throughout their lives, it is not unusual for the concept referred to as "God" to evolve also. As this happens, there can be a turning away from concepts previously held as one evolves toward a deeper, truer understanding of, and relationship with, this Mystery.

For this reason, I will seldom use the term "God" because many awakening people can't relate to it. This does not mean I don't have a deep appreciation for the Divine Mystery and those beings such as Jesus who have so strikingly embodied it. I simply mean that the Divine Mystery is both the Unmanifest Source and manifest substance of All That Is, by whatever name anyone wishes to refer to It.

What has become unmistakably evident to me and to my friends is that the Mystery is not just "out there" somewhere, but is everywhere arising as everything that we can see or experience—including ourselves. Everything is intimately interrelated and not actually separate. We humans have a wondrous capacity to become fully aware of our own divine nature—the manner in which we are an inseparable aspect of this one amazing Mystery. And when that occurs, it brings about a number of subtle shifts in what we might call the "ground of Being"—the foundation upon which we live our lives. No longer feeling so separate, we become paradoxically aware of being of *the same essence* as the ultimate divine Mystery, as well as all phenomena, including each other, much as a ray of sunlight is of *the same essence* as the sun. In this self-aware condition, we simply are *divinely human*.

In using this term I do not mean to offend anyone who feels that claiming one's divinity is heresy. I am not saying "I am God" except in the manner that such a statement also applies to you and to everyone. I am not saying that those who are *divinely human* are more godly than anyone else—they are simply more fully conscious of the Mystery that is at play here in human form, and are able to hold more levels of their experience in their awareness at the same time. Plus, they tend to radiate that ineffable essence in a way that can be catalytic for others.

Being *divinely human* does not do away with or replace an appreciation for the Ultimate Mystery, and in fact typically increases the wonder, awe, devotion, and gratitude we feel for That. At least this is so for me. However, each awakening body does so in its own manner, with its own ever-evolving set of sensitivities, understandings, and descriptions. Therefore, I do not attempt to tell you what "God" is or isn't, nor how to relate to the Mystery. I leave that to each of you to discover in your own unfolding way.

1

The Darkness Before Dawn

Our Story: We hit a place in our lives—for some of us after years of self-improvement and spiritual practices—when we began to run out of steam, as we noticed that our lives were still marked by confusion, separateness, self-doubt, perhaps even despair. Yet we still hungered for something intangible that would bring meaning to our lives, something that would make it all okay.

In other words, we were in a profound "dark night of the whole being." The fulfillment we had expected from all our hard work just wasn't coming true for us. This darkness is a painful passage, but it is not a dead end: instead, it is the harbinger of a most glorious dawn.

Quiet desperation

Into every evolving life there comes a time when the strategies that normally carry you through the day—the "I'm fine" aspect of how you deal with everything coming at you—slip a little. Maybe your life feels flat, or maybe you've come to the point where it feels like your life isn't working any more. Your heart isn't in the meaningless routine of daily life or the empty encounters with your colleagues. You're discouraged about where your life is at and who you've become (or haven't become). The shiny dreams you once held are faded and dry.

Outwardly your life may be going along pretty well, with the normal sorts of daily challenges and upsets, and overall, nothing is too bad. On the other hand, your life may have been ripped asunder by events that have taken you fully to the mat, stripped you down and left you bleeding and begging for relief. In either case, the common element is a sense of "this isn't what I thought my life was supposed to be."

It may be that your winning formula just isn't working as well as it once did, or perhaps there has been a major crisis or breakdown in some area, be it professional or family-related. Or it might be in the area of your spiritual life, as you notice that what was once rich and meaningful has grown empty, or you've lost interest somehow. It might even be that you are feeling frustrated and discouraged that you have not been able to complete and stabilize an awakening, in spite of your best efforts to do so. If any of this rings true for you, you may be experiencing the darkness before dawn.

A fall from grace

For some people, this "dark night" comes after a time when they have had a rich life full of spiritual meaning. They have had one, or many, profound openings where another dimension of life was revealed. They may have felt themselves to be in direct communication with the divine, in whatever form was especially meaningful to them, such as a personal savior, some other deity or avatar, spirit guides, totems, nature spirits, or formless emptiness full of grace or Presence. Whether just a glimpse or a whole series of such encounters, the sense of being connected directly with the divine suffuses life with particular significance, and also makes the person who is experiencing such contact feel very special, as if they have been singled out for a type of direct communion. They may receive guidance that directs their lives in certain ways, that gives them a sense of purpose, or perhaps gives them unique status within their spiritual communities, as they communicate the revelations they are receiving from Spirit.

If these lines of rich inner communion are broken off, or if the access to deep sublime states becomes unavailable, it can precipitate a wholesale plunge into one of the darkest, bleakest experiences ever reported by humans, the classic "dark night of the soul." In this most difficult passage, you feel painfully abandoned by the very One whose light and peace had been your sustenance, your rudder, and a mainstay of your identity itself. And it's only natural to wonder what you have done to offend this One, to become unworthy of grace.

Running on empty

But not everyone experiences this passage in this fashion. Some people have little sense of inner connectedness with a transcendent dimension, but nevertheless are ripe for a profound, whole-being transformation. The dark time (or "Rot" in Saniel Bonder's terms) seems to affect people who are ready (whether they know it or not) for a life change, and it affects all levels of their lives—the practical and emotional, as well as the existential. One way or another, a primary symptom is that you find yourself running out of steam. In the face of systems breaking down, something in you is still prodding you toward action: take a course, start a new hobby, find a new relationship, get into therapy, do another self-help workshop, find a new spiritual teacher, or whatever. But something else, even stronger, is whispering that it won't make any difference this time, that there isn't anything you can do to fix this. And as you hear this inner voice of doubt, you may find yourself deeply discouraged, even despairing of life ever delivering the fulfillment you had once hoped for.

Something in you feels *wrong* and you're beginning to think that nothing can make a difference. You may have been given rosy pictures by teachers or gurus who implied that if you just followed their program, everything would work out right in your life. If you only thought positively (for instance), or learned the secrets, you would create the life of your dreams, and happiness and abundance would easily follow. Or if you were diligent in your meditation practice, you would awaken into a permanent state of peace and equanimity, and the normal ups and downs of human existence would trouble you no more.

But now, in spite of giving it a good try, you may be starting to feel doubt and disillusionment. In those moments when you're not blaming yourself for failing to be a good learner, you suspect that your expectations have been overblown. You might think you were led on by an unscrupulous teacher, and you're not happy about that. Or perhaps your teacher or teachers had the best of intentions, but there's still something they haven't addressed, something that leaves you feeling incomplete. If your teachers haven't delivered for you, the last thing you're wanting now is yet another teacher telling you what you should do to make everything okay.

For some people this phase comes quietly with few outer symptoms. Perhaps they find themselves questioning their spiritual beliefs, as life brings information that doesn't tally with those beliefs. Or it may come as an irresistible desire to discover what is *real*, along with a stripping away of everything that doesn't feel true anymore.

For others, this inner unraveling is accompanied by outer chaos and disintegration. Affairs happen and marriages run into trouble. Or there is loss of job, or home, or friendships, or the death of dearly loved ones. It may be that the inner loss of faith makes it nearly impossible to keep on pretending that everything's okay, or to keep doing what you've been doing. In the backwash of that, there is major upheaval in the outer reality of your life.

Not all life crises, certainly, are the darkness before dawn— the passage that leads to final, irrevocable awakening. As you read the descriptions above, you may be nodding your head and saying, "yup, been there." Everyone goes through tough times at some point in their life, but even if you are in a very dark place, that place is not **this** specific, existential dark night unless the symptoms are of a larger unraveling. However, most people experiencing a "mid-life crisis" are dancing on the edge of this opportunity for major transformation, and if they will only pay attention and cooperate with this natural process, they have the potential to come out the other side with an unprecedented spiritual enlivenment of their whole being.

A painful passage

It's very easy during this passage to feel like you are failing, or that you are not doing enough. When things are falling apart, your survival can appear threatened, and sometimes that sense of threat intensifies the inner critical voice. Sounding much like an inner parent or authority figure, when things aren't going smoothly, our inner critic automatically kicks in and begins telling us what we're doing wrong or should change. Typically, this inner voice is negative, judgmental, and shaming. And when people find themselves in the life shift that begins with the strip-down of their internal structures, this voice can become nearly relentless.

Part of the problem is that we simply don't understand what's happening to us. Here's a useful analogy: when a caterpillar reaches a certain size, complex hormonal changes begin signaling it to weave itself into a cocoon, wherein its cell structures literally melt into "caterpillar soup." If this caterpillar were human, we can easily imagine that it would feel terrified at the changes happening to it. It might even feel that it has failed, because it doesn't know how it's all going to turn out. But before too long, new structures form and one day the cocoon suddenly opens and the lovely butterfly emerges. There was an intelligence guiding the entire process, but it wasn't easy to see until the butterfly was born.

In a similar fashion, many people today are outgrowing their old psycho-emotional patterning. Their very Soul-nature is stirring awake, and it needs more room to move, express, and have greater life. The old structures begin to weaken, to make way for this new life. To a person who doesn't know what's going on, it may feel like failure, but if the larger design could be seen, this phase is just the beginning of a transformation no less profound than the metamorphosis of that caterpillar into a butterfly.

Let's take a closer look at what's really going on.

A model for human development: embodied awakening in four stages

There are many maps of spiritual progress that have been presented over the past century or so, describing three, four, seven, eight or more stages. While they don't always line up exactly, the general evolutionary trend is similar: greater complexity leads to greater freedom from fixed habits of perception and greater access to unlimited or "spiritual" frameworks. As if moving from solid to liquid to vapor to emptiness, each stage describes reality from a different orientation.

To keep things simple, I will use a four-stage model based on the development, and then higher integration, of our three primary "energy bodies." An energy body is an intelligent, self-organizing matrix with specific capacities and ways of organizing information. The three primary energy bodies are gross (physical/emotional), subtle (mental/psychic), and causal (spiritual/formless). Development proceeds sequentially from gross to subtle to causal, depending on which energy body is most activated (unfolded) at the time. Beyond the causal stage is a fourth stage, where all of the bodies come into greater alignment and coherence.

It is important to make a distinction here between *states* and *stages*. There are many states of consciousness available to humans, the most familiar being waking, dreaming, and deep sleep. There are also super-ordinary states (peak experiences), altered states induced by drugs, and trained states that are reached through meditation practices, including Witnessing and non-dual Onlyness. One hallmark of a state is that it is ephemeral, arising and passing much like the changing weather. Another characteristic of states is that many of them are available to people at any *stage* of growth. For example, even a baby experiences the states of waking, dreaming, and deep sleep, although the content of his or her experience may be fairly rudimentary. This is because the three primary energy bodies, and the states of consciousness associated with them, are present in latent form in everyone with basic human capacities.

A stage, on the other hand, is a developmental progression that proceeds organically through greater levels of complexity and inclusivity. Just as children develop increasing cognitive ability and skill as they mature into adulthood, so too do human beings develop increasing spiritual ability as they progress through the stages of spiritual unfoldment. For temporary states and glimpses to become stable capacities requires the person's subtle nervous system to have developed the ability to sustain a higher level of bio-spiritual "current," or perception, on a steady basis.

An individual's *identity-gravity*, or sense of self, will be located in the energy body that is most fully developed, or unfolded, and this unfoldment will be sequential, beginning with gross and moving to subtle, then causal. It is not possible to skip any stage of development—even though it is possible to visit a higher stage for a brief glimpse of the perspective there.

Here is the general pattern of movement through the stages of embodied awakening:

1) a glimpse or intuition of the next stage, a *hungering for more*,

2) a dark night or rotting out of identification with the structures of the current stage,

3) oscillations into and out of an expanded self-sense, foreshadowing a permanent shift,

4) awakening, or shift of identity-gravity into the new stage,

5) integration of the new perspectives with the previously developed capacities—this can be a major restructuring of the whole being,

6) a plateau or resting within the new stage, which might include revisiting an earlier stage for further development.

This pattern appears to be repeated with each of the major stage-shifts. The particular occurrences described above may be distinct or subtle, depending upon all the myriad elements in play in any individual's life at the time.

Some people will spend their entire life in the first stage, some will undergo one major transformative shift in their lifetime, and others may progress fairly rapidly through all of the stages or even beyond. It's possible that some people come into this life having fully integrated a stage in a previous lifetime, thus enabling them to mature fairly directly into a more complex stage without spending significant time in a simpler one.

The Stages of Embodied Awakening— a working model

Stage 1: In the first stage, identity-gravity lies in the gross physical/emotional energy body. There is a strong sense of being a separate self (or ego) and there is strong identification with the body and its feelings and reactions. The main focus tends to be on issues of survival, sexuality, family, traditions, and personal accomplishment. The attitude at this stage is often one of being a **victim**, of being "done to," resulting in blaming others and/or a higher power for what happens. If the person is religious, they may sense "God" as a mysterious, unfathomable, and all-powerful Other, a holy Father that feels separate or remote from their personal experience. Since the divine presence cannot yet be felt internally, it is taken on faith, and the holy text of whatever the person's religion may be is interpreted literally. Conventional religion primarily addresses this stage. In the chakra system, this stage would energetically correlate with activation of the first three chakras.

The dark night experience that follows Stage 1 has been called the dark night of the senses. Primary identity-gravity in the body and sensory experience (a material/mechanistic view of the world) is being unwound in order to open the way for a spiritual renewal. This dark night may correlate with the "bottoming out" experience of alcoholics and addicts that is addressed by welcoming them into a spiritual program such as the 12 steps of Alcoholics Anonymous.

Stage 2: In the second stage, identity-gravity shifts to the subtle mental/psychic energetic body and the sense of self resides more fully with the conceptual mind. There is a growing ability for abstract or metaphorical thinking, and a growing awareness of subtle states or feelings. Humanistic, rational, or agnostic approaches may become dominant at this stage, leading people to reject the religion of their youth in favor of a more "scientific" worldview, though there may also be a growing interest in New Age psychic development, mysticism, and cultivation of the inner intuitive world. Issues of cultural identity, communication, and relationship are important. The focus at this stage is one of **empowerment**—discovering one's ability to create or to "manifest" the results one desires through visualization, affirmation, and intention. In religious terms, the development of subtle senses leads to a growing capacity for noticing a spark of divinity within, which may be heard as a still small voice. Or else it may appear as spirit guides, totems, deities, or other forms of the divine that can be interacted with in a direct, personal manner, leading one to feel especially chosen for such attention. This stage energetically correlates with activation of the 4th, 5th, and 6th chakras.

The dark night experience that follows Stage 2 has been called the dark night of the soul, or (in cases of embodied awakenings) dark night of the whole being. The primary attachment to and identification with the subtle body and psychic experiences, as well as residual attachment to the body and emotions, is being deconstructed. This can be an acutely painful passage, often described as feeling abandoned by Spirit and left adrift in one's life without a rudder. Although unpleasant, this step is necessary if one is to fully awaken the divine within, and it is this particular passage that I call the darkness before dawn.

Stage 3: In the third stage, or *divinely human awakening*, identity-gravity shifts to encompass the causal/spiritual energetic body *and the personal self*, both. There is a deepening sense of self as a spiritual being, leading to a marriage or joining of the awakening divine *Soul* with the personal human *self*. The divine, which was personified as a remote God in Stage 1 and became a personal divine Friend or "spark of divinity within" at Stage 2, is now realized to be none other than your own true inner Essence (or Soul-nature) which now begins to awaken and express itself as your authentic whole-being Self. In contrast to the development of personal power in Stage 2, a hallmark of Stage 3 is the quality of **surrendering** to something more powerful than your personal self, while also learning to relax into and trust Being. Divine Consciousness comes steadily on-line as Presence—the compassionate witness of all arising phenomena. Unlike the traditional description of Witnessing as aloof from the personal self (which might happen for a while prior to dropping into embodiment) the embodied witnessing of Presence happens from within, right in the midst of the human experience, which is fully permitted and embraced. There is a sense of one's true essence arriving, or landing, fully in the body—of finally being *here*. This brings a quality of **paradox** as divine and human are united and the ability to experience reality as simultaneously unfettered *and* bound comes on board, with a novel both/and quality becoming the norm. This stage energetically correlates with activation of the 7th chakra. The opening of the crown permits the bio-spiritual current to fully *enter and inhabit* the personal self beginning with the divine Heart, and from there, the whole being. While there may be experiences of unity with all phenomena at this stage, identity-gravity tends to remain primarily with the individuated self, which has the challenge now of learning to navigate life as a divinely human being.

Stage 4: Beyond Stage 3, there is a more complete merger, or fusion of, divine, human, and world into a sense of seamless Onlyness. Beyond all states of consciousness, the ineffable ground of Being is finally realized through direct gnosis or apperception, and that ground is seen to be the source and substance of everything, and every activity, in the phenomenal realm. Including us! This **integral** stage tends to develop gradually as a result of greater synthesis among the three primary energy bodies, and brings with it a capacity for deep listening and genuine compassion—both for one's self and for others—knowing how very difficult it is to fully *be here* as a conscious, sensitive, loving person. Any dark night experience (if there is one, which isn't necessarily the case) before this shift would most likely involve the final unwinding of the primary identification with a separate self-sense, in order to permit a full release into the formless ground of Being.

The realization of Onlyness found at this stage is the recognition that *there is nothing that is not divine*—at this level all opposites fuse into indivisible unity. Subjectively, there is a continual experience of the divine ground of Being at all times coupled with the entire range of possible human experience, without restriction or undue concern. At this stage, one knows oneself to BE the cosmic mystery—completely inseparable from it, and of the same essential nature—more fully than ever before. Without trying to transcend or otherwise rid oneself of egoic patterns, this stage organically softens the edges of the ego-boundaries enough that the defensive structures begin to melt away, leaving a kind of radiant beauty in their wake. More and more the personality is being transformed into a vehicle for divine expression through the action of Consciousness itself as it comes ever more fully into embodied existence.

A Caveat

This map cannot do justice to the unique way that every awakening person, including you, will come into their own spiritual unfoldment. In lived reality, there is far more variability of sequence than I have represented here. It is not unusual for someone who is still, fundamentally, in the second or third stage of unfoldment to have a profound experience of the formless ground of Being, just as some people seem to come into a realization of Onlyness without having had a knock-your-socks-off experience of formless Consciousness. This of course makes the whole project of trying to help someone recognize their stage of development pretty confusing. So be it—Consciousness is still evolving and we are all learning as we go. This map is just a pointer, a means of helping you understand the shifts that may already be underway in you.

In summary

As you grow and evolve, you are unfolding more and more of the inherent potentials of your divinely human self. In order to make way for the next level of complexity (and therefore an expanded range of potential experience), the old structures and patterns you have grown familiar with will be deconstructed. Your very sense of how you see yourself and manage your life may undergo radical transformation, just as a caterpillar undergoes inside its cocoon.

This is primarily an inner process, although some people find that it affects their outer lives as well. It is not necessary for your life to fall apart in order for you to awaken! What does seem to be a necessary precursor, however, is that you're at least beginning to question "how you've always been" or "what you've always believed is so." When you question in this manner, or realize that you don't really know all the answers, something new becomes possible.

Presented here is a map that certainly oversimplifies the very complex dynamic of human spiritual growth and evolution, but it is a starting point to help you get oriented to what may be going on inside you. Remember that what looks at first like defeat, or failure, may actually be the first sign of a growing readiness for something new, something that will give your life a totally different ground from which to grow and thrive. We could say that the dark night phase is a sign of your deepest essence coming out of its dormancy and stirring to life—because a passage like this is the very thing that opens the door for a new type of integrated awareness to arise. This is an organic process that has its own intelligence. Gradually, over time, that "no more energy for doing anything about it" feeling that accompanies the darkness before dawn shows us that we can let go of much of our effort and just *relax*. Then we begin to discover a different basis for our lives, one that welcomes all of what we are—for it is only when all the aspects, or energy bodies, of our humanness are integrated that we can fully experience our birthright: profound wellness of Being.

How to know if you are in the dark night

Here are some signs* that you might be rotting out of your old frameworks and preparing yourself (albeit unconsciously) for a transformation. You may recognize yourself in one or more of them, and some of these may apply more than others:

- You're not interested in trying any more self-help programs
- You aren't looking for a guru, or another teacher
- You suspect that what you've been told in the past was inaccurate, or not sufficient to what you're dealing with now
- You're questioning all your beliefs
- You've gotten less consistent about, or even discontinued, your spiritual practice (and perhaps feel guilty about that)
- You feel alone, as if no one understands what you're going through
- You hesitate to speak about your challenges, because the typical response is for your listener to suggest some program or therapy to fix what ails you—and you're done with all that
- You're heart-sick (or feel betrayed) because you've lost the sense of profound connection with Spirit that you once had
- Or you feel discouraged because, while you intermittently feel a deep sense of connection, you can't sustain it in the midst of your reactivity to daily life challenges

---

* Note that some of these symptoms may also be those of clinical depression or a physical disorder, so if the quality of your life is being significantly downgraded, please consult a professional (trusted medical doctor or psychotherapist) for assistance.

- Your old strategies for winning favor in the world aren't working for you now
- Your ability to use positive thinking to change your feelings or your life circumstance isn't working as well as it once did
- You feel hopeless about ever finding lasting peace, or enlightenment
- You feel like a failure, or a disappointment
- You're just plain tired at the core
- You don't feel you're in control of your life anymore
- You feel a longing, deep down, to awaken and discover your true nature, and that longing just won't go away

The importance of good company

Throughout history, some people have had the ability to awaken and reconnect strongly with Being or Source, and at the beginning of the 21st century, their numbers appear to be on the rise. Their words sometimes carry a special power, and the quality of their Presence is often catalytic to those around them who are receptive to it. It's really helpful at this point to meet up with others who have been through this passage and know what's on the other side, who are radiating the confidence that comes from this new understanding through their very essence. We call this radiating essence "transmission," and it is the topic of the next chapter.

2

INITIATORY ENCOUNTERS

Our Story: Through exposure to the teachings and transmission of a divinely human person, who, by his or her very existence, revealed the possibility of a truly different way of facing the challenges of being human, changes began happening in us. We felt enlivened by this contact, and began to feel ourselves responding with renewal of hope.

Subtle communication

Below the threshold of thought, words, or physical expression, there is a subtle communication that takes place body-to-body in any encounter. It is as if the fundamental condition of the whole being telegraphs itself outward, and other bodies receive and understand that communication. When this phenomenon occurs between an awakened person and one who is aspiring to awaken, it is called "transmission." It's a bit like running your finger along the top of a crystal glass. When the glass begins to ring, other similar glasses nearby may also begin ringing, even though they have not been touched, because they are in resonance with—receptive to—the ringing glass.

There are different types of transmission in different spiritual traditions. Some are quite transcendent; when you are in the field of transcendence you may find yourself becoming very internally quiet and blissful. The ordinary cares of the world fade into the background, and the chattering of the mind lessens, leaving you feeling quite peaceful. In this internally quiet condition, it may be easier for your Conscious nature to become apparent to you.

Embodied, or *divinely human* transmission, on the other hand, encompasses the entire range of our humanness—mind, body, and emotions, as well as transcendent Consciousness. This leads to a here-now grounded quality that's distinctly different from more transcendent types of transmission, which put more emphasis on rising above (or dropping beneath) experience than on the physicality of embodiment. When you are in the field of embodied transmission, you may experience an intensification of *any* aspect of your experience because nothing is being excluded. Everything is welcomed and embraced. In particular, YOU are welcomed, exactly as you are in this moment.

Embodied transmission is based on trust and confidence in Being, among other things. Trust in Being comes from deeply knowing that it is possible to live the paradox of being both fully divine and fully human at the same time, and it is this knowing that is being radiated, effortlessly, all the time by people who are stabilized in their embodied awakenings. Though this paradox is inexplicable to the recipient's rational mind, the body and whole being *can* and *do* understand, intuitively.

The lineage of embodiment

The living fire of conscious embodiment is something that passes from body to body like a flame passes from a lit candle to an unlit one. In many traditional spiritual paths, emphasis is given to the lineage of the current leaders: "So-and-so was my teacher, and his teacher was so-and-so" back through generations of lineage-holders who have a certain type of transmission in common.

In embodied awakenings, things are unfolding somewhat differently. Saniel Bonder, the originator of Waking Down in Mutuality, had been a disciple of Adi Da and had imbibed his particular type of embodied transmission. But Saniel was not awakened or acknowledged by Adi Da, and instead experienced the shift into embodied awakening after leaving Adi Da and becoming a "free agent." Saniel does have a lineage, yet his transmission is uniquely his own.

Saniel's embodied transmission drew together an eclectic group of practitioners, and many of them had no experience of Adi Da or the Hindu traditional path. So, as they in turn awakened and became teachers, they added their own "lineages" (personal history and spiritual paths they had already experienced) into the mix. Today, this community of divinely human people is a blend of many different lineages as well as a "wild" spontaneous element. The transmission from each divinely human teacher is individual and unique in some ways, yet the basis of it will always be the seamless Onlyness of our divinely human embodiment that embraces everything and rejects nothing.

Gazing meditation

Transmission does not require physical proximity. It can also occur through written words, photographs, recorded words or videos, over telephone lines, or even when sitting in silent meditation with someone many miles away. But, when possible, body-to-body encounters can be especially catalytic.

Gazing is a particularly potent means of transmission that stimulates both awakening and deep healing. In gazing, the teacher makes gentle eye contact with the student. It is a form of direct meeting that bypasses the normal verbal level of communication, so the mind is less engaged and the heart is more likely to be touched. In gazing, the teacher's Presence is vibrating strongly, providing an opportunity for the participant to begin vibrating in a similar fashion. Or, in other words, the teacher's state of Presence is seeing and calling Presence forward in the student, so that it can become an integrated, whole-being experience for them as well.

At workshops, sittings (group gatherings with a teacher), or private sessions, gazing meditation is an important part of an embodied teacher's offering to their students. It is not necessary for the student to do anything or to have a particular attitude in order for gazing to be effective, since it is doing its magic underneath the surface. The range of experiences reported by students is quite large, from "didn't feel anything at all" to "deep shame" to "my heart was blown wide open" and all points in between. Each and every gazing session is unique—sometimes ordinary, sometimes notable—but the stimulation of this form of communication continues to work its gentle magic whether anything is registered by the conscious mind or not.

Gazing is primal. Gazing between a mother and her baby is essential for normal human development, as it calls the baby's spirit forward into initial embodiment and mutual interaction. In similar fashion, gazing meditation can also be a potent "calling forward" of the adult's awakening spirit into greater embodiment and relatedness in mutuality.

Seeing and being seen

Most of us have a deep hunger to be really *seen* as who we are, in a loving and compassionate fashion that acknowledges our inner beauty and all the struggles we have faced—and currently face— simply being here as a human being. Being here is no cake-walk. It is a rare person whose parents were able to fully see and welcome them as divinely human beings, so what you probably experienced was a mixture that included praise for acting the way your parents wanted, and criticism or punishment for deviating from that. The times you were acknowledged for simply being *yourself* might have been few and far between. You may not even have much of a sense of what "being yourself" would look or feel like.

If what you encountered was more on the side of judgment and criticism than welcoming embrace, you might have developed a deep *fear* of being seen—especially of being called out or revealed or publicly shamed. Your true, essential nature may have gone into hiding from early on. All too many children have to cope with parents who are having a hard time navigating their own human life—parents who may act irrationally or even violently toward their children at times without warning. If you were raised in such an environment, you probably built some walls around your tender essence to keep it from being totally crushed.

Even for those raised in a fairly benign environment, personalities tend to develop more in line with conforming to parental (and teacher and peer) expectations than as the expression of true nature. While this has adaptive survival value, it doesn't allow for much in the way of authentic self-expression, which is the desire of every soul. Deep down, there lives a hope that one day you will be able to shed outdated aspects of your personality that aren't authentic for you, and begin shining forth as the divinely human Self that you truly are.

The simple act of gazing with a teacher may trigger issues from past experiences, positive or negative, of having been seen or not seen by others. This is normal and there is nothing that needs to "be done" about it. You can just breathe into it and allow the feelings to be there as they will. Take it at your own pace and participate at whatever level you find comfortable. It is perfectly acceptable, for instance, to make brief eye contact and then close your eyes; not pushing yourself beyond what feels right in the moment.

Most people discover pretty quickly that gazing is a loving experience which speaks to the deepest part of them, beyond the mind. And they may notice that something in them gets touched in a way that is rare and special, and that the shyest, most tender part of who they are is welcomed to come forth here, where it is most safe to do so, to be seen and recognized and nurtured into wholeness.

Initiation

When you think of initiation, you might think of a ritual or rite of passage. "Initiate" also means to begin something—to enter into a new phase of your life. When you land in the darkness before dawn, it may feel as if something in you is dying or ending—which it is. That which no longer reflects and serves who you truly are is dying in order to make way for something new, something more authentic. And when you meet someone who can give you a positive framework for what is going on in you, especially if she or he also transmits a remarkably grounded confidence in Being, something significant may be catalyzed in you. It is your own inner essence stirring, waking from its slumber. You are being initiated into the next great stage of your own spiritual unfoldment.

Sometimes such an initiation will feel expansive, freeing, and blissful, as if your heart and whole being were opening wide. All the stress, tension, and anxiety you have been feeling begins to melt away and a deep sense of wellness arises throughout your whole being. There may be a renewal of hope, with a sense of new possibilities opening up for you, and you might feel "high" for days or weeks, with a new influx of creativity and inspiration.

On the other hand, an initiation may just as likely come with an increased feeling of contraction or pain, as if your internal pressure had been turned up high and is now squeezing all of your most tender places. You might have feelings of unworthiness, or perhaps your inner critical voice is off and running with all the reasons this isn't going to work for you and you're going to fail— once again. Or you may find yourself reliving earlier painful incidents of your life, perhaps accompanied by feelings of guilt, shame, or sorrow.

In *both* cases, the underlying dynamic is one of increased energy and internal activity, a "heating up" of your whole being. Something in you that has been lying dormant is coming alive, unfurling itself just like those butterfly wings I spoke of in the last chapter. And this coming alive will inevitably lead, in turn, to further unfoldment, new discoveries, and greater aliveness on all levels of your total self.

Heart openings and other surprises

Initial contact with an open-hearted person who sees you as the divinely human person you are becoming may cause your own heart to open in response. You might experience strong feelings of love and devotion arising, directed toward the one who has served you in this way. You may even find yourself falling in love with them.

These feelings are a normal part of embodied awakening. They are not required, certainly, for transmission to have its most auspicious effect, and they may never arise in that fashion, but for many people they do. It is rare in this world for people to stop and connect fully, seeing one another in their full divinely human beauty. Our most significant experiences of love, other than the bonding of mother and baby, typically happen when we fall in love with someone and our defenses drop away for a while, leaving us deliciously open to a rare depth of intimacy. So it is no wonder that if you experience something similar in a meeting with a teacher, you might interpret what's happening in ways that are familiar from prior experience. The special gift of this type of heart-opening is that it temporarily takes you outside of your old, habitual ways of experiencing yourself, and allows you to see yourself freshly, through the other's eyes. They are seeing your inner divinity, and when you are open to it, you will begin to see it, too.

If feelings like these arise, try to allow yourself to enjoy them without making too much of them. In Chapter 7, I will go further into the dynamics of working with a teacher for your most auspicious unfoldment into your divinely human potential.

Divinely human teachers are divinely *human*

If you have an expectation that an awakened teacher is somehow immune to or above the sorts of human messiness that ordinary people experience, you may be disappointed when you discover that Consciously-embodied teachers are still subject to ordinary human emotions, thoughts, feelings, and reactions.

There are some fundamental differences, of course, from unawakened human experience, but the freedom such teachers enjoy comes from surrendering *into* the human condition rather than bypassing or suppressing it.

If you see them angry, sad, fearful, or reactive, you may experience confusion or internal conflict. Divinely human teachers don't hold any of those conditions as essentially bad, wrong or less desirable than conditions of ease and peacefulness, which they also experience. And unlike professional therapists, most embodied spiritual teachers do not withhold their personal experience from their students. They are willing to let you to see how it is for them, what it's really like to live this strange paradox of human divinity so that you can recognize that you do not have to do away with the feelings, emotions, and thoughts that make up your humanness in order to awaken.

Some spiritual teachers, especially those from eastern traditions, keep a certain distance from their students. It is easier, in this situation, for the teacher to appear more "together" than might actually be revealed if they were around all the time, day in and day out. In contrast, divinely human teachers typically do not try to present themselves as perfected and pristine because they don't feel that it serves you in the long run. It's too easy in those cases for students to assume a higher level of perfection than is actually the case, and to conclude that they can't awaken until they are also perfected.

What is far more likely is that you will find yourself awakening just as you are—warts and all. If you "take a mug shot" of who you now are, in all your wonderful imperfection, well, that's who is awakening here. It's not that you won't change and evolve—you will—but you won't likely have completed your purification before significant, profound shifts begin to occur. It's actually one of the myths of enlightenment that you have to spend years perfecting yourself before any significant awakening can happen. Perhaps that was true in the past, but we've seen hundreds of people just like you (and me) popping through into a profound realization of their fundamental nature long before they thought they were ready or worthy. And once that embodied wholeness takes root, divinely human realizers can begin transmitting their embodied wholeness for others even as they are still evolving themselves.

And who can say what they are evolving into? One thing that seems certain is that divinely human people continue to experience the whole range of human feelings and emotions, from bliss to occasional despair and back again. The "divinely human experiment" is still itself evolving, revealing body by body what is possible and desirable for human transformation.

If you are hoping that awakening is going to take away your ordinary, messy humanness, and if you are hoping that your teacher will be a paragon of seamless equanimity, your "where's the perfection?" button will likely be pushed before too long. But don't underestimate embodied teachers. Hundreds of seekers have already awakened into a permanent, irrevocable condition of Conscious embodiment through the path of Waking Down in Mutuality. Relaxing right *into* the human condition is one of the secrets that have made this work so very effective, and we'll explore that more deeply in Chapter 3.

Due diligence

You do not have to believe, or take on face value, everything (or anything) written or spoken by a divinely human person. Please bring an open mind to how you read this book, and to any meetings you have, and then see if this approach speaks to who you are and what is going on in your process. It's possible that the embodied approach might not be right for you at this time, but will be at another time when you are in a different phase of your unfoldment. It's especially useful for people who are unraveling, as in the darkness before dawn, and for people who find themselves already awakening and hoping to find others who understand what's happening to them.

Tanking up

If you are thirsty for the nectar of awakening, then by all means come and tank up! Find ways to avail yourself of transmission in its various forms. Get into the room with divinely human others whenever you can, and when that's not possible, get on the phone for private sessions or group conference calls. You can read the writings of embodied teachers, listen to music they have created, behold their artwork, or watch videos of them teaching. Many people enjoy video gazing, as well, so I have posted a gazing video for you at **divinelyhuman.com**, and a gazing photo at the end of this book.

There are many ways to receive inspiration and support for your awakening process. However, there's no substitute for someone who is living in seamless integration of the transcendent divine with their embodied humanness, who can transmit that to you in such a way that you can template off of them into your own embodied awakening. This is something that they do effortlessly, 24/7, simply because they are living and being it. Whether they appear to be in an exalted state and deeply peaceful, or agitated and reacting to something in their environment, the simple truth is that they are embodying Onlyness by consciously embracing whatever is arising in them in the moment, and they're doing it in such a way that it gets transmitted energetically to receptive others. And chances are good that they most sincerely wish to support you into becoming divinely human as well.

I'll have more to say about seeking out and utilizing support on your journey in Chapter 7. First, it's important to understand how the stress of the human predicament causes *dis*-tress when it is not understood or not yet brought into full awareness. The healing possible with embodied awakening, while not removing the stress entirely, relieves much of its pain. I'll be discussing this more fully in the next chapter.

3

Relaxing into the Core Wound

Our Story: We were frustrated and disappointed that our efforts at self-improvement had brought only limited results. We couldn't fully control ourselves, our lives, or the world around us, no matter how hard we tried to follow the programs or teachings that were supposed to relieve us of the feelings of dissatisfaction, unhappiness, or "not-enoughness" at the core of our being. Once we realized that this "core wound" was the natural and inescapable result of the basic human predicament—intuiting that we are Infinite Souls but experiencing our lives as very conditioned, limited selves—we stopped being so hard on ourselves and began to relax and trust the wisdom and intelligence of Being.

"There's something fundamentally wrong with me"

"Why can't I be more successful?"

"Why can't I get free of my self-doubt, judging, criticizing, and confusion?"

"Why do I feel so unworthy—still?"

"Why do peace, ease, and wellness seem so ephemeral?"

"If we're really all One, why do I still feel scared and alone?"

If you're like many people, you ask yourself these kinds of questions all too often. Despite your best efforts to master yourself and your life, something eludes you. You have a nagging sense that something's not right with you, and your inner critic is more than willing to point out all the ways it must be YOUR FAULT.

I invite you to reconsider that conclusion.

As human beings, we seem uniquely challenged to be content in our own skins. We often suffer from overactive minds and imaginations, intense self-criticism, crippling self-doubt, volatile emotions, unending stress, debilitating fear and/or scary rages. We have a difficult time loving ourselves, much less our neighbors, and we often bump up against painful limitations, either in our own skills and capacity or in the circumstances and people around us. Topping it off, we understand that our bodies have expiration dates, and our time here is not going to be endless. If we love, we will also sooner or later know the pain of saying goodbye to someone we have loved.

However, we also have the ability to sense or imagine our spiritual nature, that part of us that is infinite, unconditioned, and unlimited—that feels free, peaceful, impervious, spacious, and unreservedly loving of ourselves and all things. Whether we feel this directly as a part of our life experience, remember it vaguely as if from a time before birth, or simply have an intuition that it's possible, we cannot help but feel the juxtaposition of our current experience against this spacious freedom as a sort of rub, or tension at the core. This "core wound" is a fundamental condition that results when the limitations or conflicts in our lives are contrasted against an idealized sense of wholeness, ease, and grace.

Every body has a core wound, and each person will feel this core wound somewhat differently, according to their natural propensities. You might feel it as heaviness or deep sadness, or as tension that never lets up, or as pressure or heat, as if you sometimes want to jump out of your skin. Beneath these sensations, the core wound generally brings feelings of being confused in identity, separate in relatedness, or incomplete, as if you need to find or be *something more* than who and what you already are.

You might feel confused in identity if you're never quite sure of what you are: are you an animal with a large capacity for thinking, or are you a divine spiritual being having a human life?

Are you fundamentally good, or bad? Just what are you? And why do you frequently experience life as being so difficult or painful, even when your survival needs are more than sufficiently met?

You might feel a sense of separateness as if you're enclosed in a bubble, with others being forever outside of that bubble no matter how much you long for closeness and intimacy. Or you might feel cut off from God, or Source, or Spirit—however you sense that quality of the divine. If you have any intuition or remembrance of a time when that was not the case, when the walls of separation melted and there was a flow of unity and infinite spiritual wholeness, you might feel a great *angst* when that beautiful sense of connection and flow is not available or present.

Or, you might feel incomplete, and frequently think, *"There must be more than this,"* or, *"I need to be more than I am,"* because, while you are aware of your limitations, you are also aware of your potential. Life can become an endless pursuit of *more* as you try to get a better education, a better job, more recognition, better salary, better home, better car, more stuff, more trainings, more skills, better romantic partner, etc., ad infinitum— until you begin to see that these things, in and of themselves, don't really make you happy.

Or you might feel a constant nagging sense of dis-ease, as if you're somehow wrong, or bad, or unlovable, or inadequate to the demands of your life. Or perhaps you feel *afraid* that you're those things. You then make an unnecessary but reflexive leap in your thinking, and interpret the sense of not *feeling* good at the core as a sign that *you're actually* not good (or good enough)— that there's something *fundamentally wrong* with you.

Most people are not consciously aware of the core wound. Because this tension, or rub, can be quite uncomfortable, especially when it is not understood, people tend to avoid feeling it at all costs. Instead, they use all sorts of things to try to tune out this feeling. They may keep themselves very active through work, creative projects, raising kids, hobbies, sports, sex, television watching, etc., or they numb themselves through consumption of mood-altering substances. Or they may try to engender euphoria through repeatedly falling in love. In one way or another, the core wound drives much of human endeavor as people restlessly try to stay one step ahead of simply feeling it. This is why it is so uncomfortable for people to sit quietly doing nothing: they might drop into the distress at their core. I remember someone once telling me, when informed that I was about to enter a 10-day silent retreat: "I would rather die than sit in silence for a week!" Although she had never tried it, she was afraid of what she would feel if she let herself be still and quiet. Stopping the rush of life and sitting quietly is quite difficult when you don't understand what you're feeling at the core and are afraid of what you might discover there.

Core issues are not the core wound

The core wound is not the same as *core issues*. Core issues are trauma patterns that resulted from particular events or situations in our lives, usually in childhood but sometimes later on as well. A core issue can certainly bring with it feelings of distress or despair, as our current life events stimulate a reactivation of the original memories and physiological reactions. The core wound, however, lies beneath even these deep-seated configurations. Core issues are unique to each person and are related to their life story—they have a script, like "I feel insecure because my father was alcoholic and I never knew whether he'd be friendly toward me or angry and attacking." On the other hand, the core wound is universal and occurs in every human being, even those who have experienced little trauma and seem to be outwardly well-adjusted. It has a subtle feeling, but no story line. It is intrinsic to being human, and everyone has a core wound, whether they are aware of it or not.

The core wound is not your fault

Humanity has a long history of struggling with the feeling that there's something wrong or evil about human nature. Many different interpretations have been made, including the Judeo-Christian concept of original sin. The story says that at one time we lived in a state of grace, but that with the advent of free will we misused that freedom, offended God, and fell out of the state of grace. Now we are expected to atone for "our sins" in some fashion or another. This framework—that we (or our ancestors) did something wrong and need to do something to fix it—is an understandable attempt to explain the way we feel at the core, and some version of it shows up in many spiritual teachings from around the world. But it represents a fundamental misunderstanding of the core wound.

The core wound is NOT the result of something that we did wrong, nor is it something that needs to be atoned for. We are simply an evolving species that developed a remarkable capacity for conceptual thinking that we haven't yet integrated with the other parts of ourselves.

Mind-body splits

In the early days of our evolutionary trajectory we were tribal animals in a challenging physical environment, gathered together into social groups. We could say that our earliest culture tended to be organic, fluid, and generally feminine in its orientation to life. It was more right-brained, adaptive and cooperative with the natural rhythms of life than what became the norm later on.

As the human capacity for logical, linear thought expanded, we became more objective, formulaic, and masculine. There was a shift toward left-brain dominance, with its innate tendency toward modifying and controlling the environment. Our newly-arising capacity for conceptual thinking added a powerful new dimension in our ability to adapt and thrive on the planet. We began strategizing how to fix and improve our environment and our lives on many levels. We could anticipate and head off danger and we could imagine how to be more successful in endeavors of all kinds—from hunting to gardening to raising kids to building homes, and on and on. Over time, we began to focus more and more of our energy in the domain of thinking, and less in the domain of the body, emotion, and feelings.

As our capacity for conceptual thinking grew stronger, there was little understanding of how to reconcile this newer function with our already-existing instinctual/emotional behavior patterns— patterns the species had been relying on over the ages for its survival. The failure to integrate instinct, emotions, and thinking into a seamless unity led ultimately to the gap between mind and body becoming ever more exaggerated. The capacity to reflect and think speculatively about our experience also led to a greater awareness of our spiritual nature, and then with this awareness came the awareness of the core wound, that unpleasant juxtaposition of our human limits against our spiritual potential for experiencing infinity, deep peace, wellness, and freedom. Because feeling into oneself deeply might mean feeling things one would normally avoid, it was natural that people would suppress uncomfortable feelings. The useful masculine application of thinking to improve the environment we lived in then began to be distorted into exaggerated attempts to control our inner world as well—our bodies, thoughts, and emotions. Soon we began trying to override, control, or transcend our basic impulses as well as that uncomfortable feeling at the core.

As rational thought grew in stature, the cult of human mastery over nature was born. The western world entered the "age of reason" and remarkable achievements were attained using methodical, "scientific" approaches to tackling the problems of the world (though not without a price). The impulse to control the material world spilled over into control of our inner world:

- control how you think as in "think and grow rich"
- control how you feel as in "keep a stiff upper lip"
- and control your body and words as in "be a nice person."

We've been taught that we are better people if we hold back our spontaneous thoughts, feelings, and needs for expression. And while these austerities have lessened their grip in recent years, there is still a prevalent attitude that it's up to you to learn the right techniques to make your life work, and if it isn't working, you're somehow to blame.

In the eastern world, the focus was less on developing strategies to control the material world, and more about developing the ability to transcend spiritually. The stronger emphasis was put on using yogic or meditative self-discipline to develop a refined mental focus (transcendence) in order to bypass and dissociate from the baser, more instinctual aspects of our nature:

- I am not this body
- I am not these thoughts
- I am not these emotions.

Here too, the belief is that you'll be a better and more holy person if you distance yourself from your spontaneous, natural feelings and reactions. In all cases throughout this period of human evolution, there is evidence of an increasing **split** between the head and the heart—between mind and body, thinking and feeling.

This split still shows up in each of us today in our habitual ways of thinking and acting, and in particular in some basic assumptions we hold about ourselves that might not prove to be entirely true upon closer inspection. For instance, the mind projects from its ability to learn how to build a better mousetrap to thinking it can build a better person. Because it can control the environment by, for instance, turning the dial on a thermostat, it thinks it can control the inner environment by controlling what thoughts are permitted, or which emotions are felt. A huge "self-help" industry has arisen that is devoted to solving "the problem" of human emotions and feelings, in the attempt to make us all into super-achievers who feel good all the time. However, our default, patterned ways of reacting to life tend to be quite resistant to being controlled by our mind, hence we spend much of our time in inner chaos and confusion, with parts of us at war with other parts, causing much distress.

Saniel Bonder calls the tendency to apply a formulaic process to suppress our so-called negative aspects and fix and improve everything else "hypermasculine," because it is an exaggerated form of the masculine impulse to solve problems by action in the external world.

The impulse to fix ourselves (to avoid feeling pain)

No matter what the specific formula is trying to address—"10 Easy Steps to Financial Security" or "10 Easy Ways to Mend a Broken Heart"—the underlying assumption is that so-called "negative" feelings such as insecurity or pain are something that need to be fixed, or made to go away. This is due to the ancient distrust of what cannot be controlled—what is wild and spontaneous—and the impetus to press it down, tame it, or make it obey.

This is important enough to repeat: we misinterpret the distress of the core wound as a sign that there's something wrong with us, and then find ourselves automatically being motivated to *do something about it*. We become obsessed with trying to do something to make ourselves "okay." There's a huge range of what we think it will take for us to be "okay" including all levels of success, wealth, accomplishment, ideal relationships, etc., but it all ultimately boils down to what will make us okay in our own eyes (generally influenced heavily by our particular cultural conditioning).

The hypermasculine approach to life has permeated practically every aspect of human existence, and it has become our default orientation. It is a survival function run amok. "Find it and fix it" is its strategy, and it has little tolerance for anything that doesn't bow down to its control. It sets us up to be inwardly split, with some parts of ourselves rejecting or trying to control other parts, a condition of inner division that is quite painful to experience and only partially amenable to the many ways we try to alleviate it.

It is impossible to succeed more than temporarily by using a hypermasculine approach to resolving this predicament (although it is also impossible to avoid trying to do so). Any time we are shown a model for "what ails us," it is practically inevitable to ask "What do I do to change that? Give me the formula, the technique I need to apply."

We're powerless in the face of the core wound

You cannot make the core wound go away by any means, because it is simply how you are configured. It's part of being human.

To repeat: <u>you **cannot** make the core wound go away.</u>

Attempts to make it go away or to avoid feeling it ultimately fail. Just as alcohol eventually fails to provide the anesthesia it once did, so too any attempt to override or "cure" the feeling of the core wound will ultimately fall short. Such attempts are at best only temporarily successful, and there is a big price to pay in the damage we do to ourselves in the process. All suppressed feeling is stored as a form of cellular memory which will resurface repeatedly until it is allowed, felt, and permitted to heal.

An example: a little child who has been upset by something and is beginning to cry is warned by his parent, "Stop crying right now or I'll give you something to really cry about!" The boy, now also feeling fear, tenses up certain muscles in his face, shoulders, and hands and somehow shuts off the flow of tears. He is beginning to learn how to override the feeling of being upset and hold his emotions at bay. Years later, he experiences chronic tension in his face, neck, and shoulders and can't let himself cry, even when faced with great loss.

Cutting off our spontaneous thoughts, feelings, and impulses also cuts us off from our vital energy, depriving us of our very aliveness. In the attempt to avoid feeling painful feelings, we create an ever greater amount of pain and suffering for ourselves as we deplete our vitality and depress our aliveness. This is reaching a critical point in the modern world: just look at how many people are resorting to antidepressants and other drugs to try to address a serious lack of inner wellbeing.

No way out

Now you may find yourself in a classic catch-22 bind: upon discovering that you are ultimately powerless to control or escape your human predicament through your own strategic efforts, you will likely begin searching for yet another strategy you can use to undo your previous strategies. This is pretty automatic and unconscious. *It is also futile.*

This would be a good time to stop and take a breath.

*   *   *   *   *

The only way out of the habit of endlessly trying to fix what's wrong with you is for you to allow it to naturally dissolve from within. As I described in Chapter 1, at some point you find yourself simply losing the drive to keep on striving to be different, better, more successful, or enlightened. You might not be satisfied with yourself as you are, but something is pulling the rug out from under the whole endeavor of trying to get it right. And this something is the thrust of your own spiritual unfolding. You are beginning to be capable of something else.

Falling into the core wound

As your impulse to avoid and override decreases, you will find that you can let yourself *be*, bringing greater awareness into the core wound itself. You will begin falling into the core wound to an ever-greater degree. It may seem a bit strange to say you "fall into" something that's already a condition of your existence, but what I mean is that you allow yourself to consciously feel how it really is for you deep down inside yourself. When you stop always looking outward at the circumstances of your life, you naturally become more available for noticing how you feel inside. Going into the core wound may seem counterintuitive, because the natural reflex is to get away from discomfort any way you can. But experiencing your inner territory with full awareness of what you're encountering is the very act that will ultimately set you free.

Being willing to feel into the core wound is the first step. It may be that you are already feeling the core wound, but you've been thinking there is something wrong with you and that you only need the right tool to fix it, to make it go away. It can be a radical shift to allow yourself to feel that sense of *angst* WITHOUT trying to make it go away. This is what I mean by relaxing: relaxing and allowing yourself to notice what's here and how you are feeling, and to become more aware of the stories you tell yourself about what it means.

And while you are relaxing and noticing what's going on inside you, also notice all the impulses that arise to *do something*. You can begin to notice how often you seek a program or strategy that will somehow make your life better or alleviate painful feelings. You can notice all the ways in which you don't like how you feel (or even who you are) and want it to change. You can notice how quickly you reach for *something* to help you avoid feeling exactly the way you're feeling, be it alcohol, TV, exercise, food, meditation, shopping, chatting with a friend, working long hours, drugs, parties, etc. You can notice the next time you're tempted to sign up for the "next best" program that promises to make you more successful, beautiful, powerful, in control, prosperous, or whatever. You can remind yourself that what drives these impulses is less about any rewards you might get than it is about helping you avoid that disquieting feeling deep down at the core: the core wound.

The truth is, if you can avoid feeling the core wound, you will. It's not that the pain is unbearable, it's more that it simply feels irresolvable. Therefore we instinctively prefer to avoid dealing with it. The majority of people spend their lives in this pattern of avoiding the core feeling of their life. But for some, the lucky ones, the drive to stay on the surface and not go deep will wind down, and they will find themselves falling—and ultimately relaxing—into the core wound.

Fortunately, relaxing into the core wound does not mean you have to be endlessly awash in feelings of confusion, separation, or inadequacy. Once you begin unwinding from your conditioned avoidance strategies, you are naturally moving toward a more direct encounter with your fundamental Being. Remember, the key here is to relax and allow yourself to organically unfold out of your old and controlled way of operating into something else. You do not have to force anything now (in fact, more and more you'll find that you simply can't). Be as gentle on yourself as possible. It is totally okay to find a rhythm between touching in with the feelings at the core, and doing things to give yourself comfort and support during this time of transition and change.

It's HARD to be here!

The bottom line is that it's very often HARD to be here as a fully aware human being. It's challenging to be here as a human being no matter what, and it's especially hard to come fully alive to all that we are. We are full of ideals and expectations about life, and the more conscious we are, the more we have to face all the ways that life fails to be ideal. It's not utopia, it's not peaceful much of the time, it's full of conflicts and war between people, and you can't get away from the fact that animals EAT ONE ANOTHER here. Life isn't fair, and before you know it, the physical body dies. This is the indisputable truth about how life is. And we're not born accepting how things are: we quickly develop a whole set of concepts about fairness, love, safety, trust, and happy endings. We expect these things, and we suffer when they aren't the case.

It's no wonder that people often backpedal AWAY from being here about as often as they lean in, wanting to live life fully. Most people end up in some twilight zone of a surface life, not questioning things too deeply and allowing their automatic ways of being to carry them along.

But here YOU are, and if you're reading this book you're not "most people." You probably already know that you are impelled to discover what's true about yourself and about life. Like Neo in the Matrix movie, you are choosing the red pill. You are ready to give up the dream life and do whatever it takes to find out what's really going on here. In the midst of the dark night you might feel like a failure on one level, but I'll wager that on another level, you are beginning to sense that you are on a hero's journey of epic proportions.

On one hand, you may not want to know what's in store for you. On the other hand, it's important for you to know that if you choose to go down this path you will be tested. You will encounter the hell-realms of your own psyche and have to face the demons there. Awakening is not a program where you can learn A, B, and C and your life is turned around. Quite the contrary: awakening happens when you permit all that is no longer relevant to your authentic self to fall away and lie in ruins, while the phoenix of your divine essence rises into new life.

To quote from *The Way of Transformation* by Karlfried Graf Durkheim: "Only if we venture repeatedly through zones of annihilation can our contact with Divine Being, which is beyond annihilation, become firm and stable."

I am not saying this to scare you, but only to level with you. If you are rotting out of your conditioned, hypermasculine ways of being, you are already in the midst of this process of total transfiguration. You do not need to enroll; life has already drafted you into this program.

Does the core wound ever get healed?

By now, you're probably wondering if there is going to be any relief, ever, from the pain of the core wound. Well, the short answer is "yes." Much of the distress of the wound comes from our resistance to it—the way we dislike and try to rid ourselves of it. Once we consciously understand its existential nature—once we really get that it's not a sign of personal failing—and accept that it's just how it feels to be in a body, then our relaxation around all that can bring us a great relief. This relaxation is a precursor to the shift of divinely human awakening, which in turn brings with it a profound wellness of Being, in which the core wound is transformed into the alchemical Core Mystery of conscious embodiment.

As long as you have a body you will always experience some degree of tension between the limits of embodiment and the freedom of Spirit. Part of awakening is learning how to live with this tension without it being so painful, and this book is here to give you tools and tips to help you do just that.

Try this: sensing inward

Here's an experiment you can try. Right now, notice how your body feels. Tune into the feeling of your chair supporting you, and then notice the feeling of contact from your clothes on your skin. Then let your awareness go down into your feet, and into the palms of your hands. You might like to take a nice full breath, and notice any sense of enlivenment that comes with that.

Next, bring your awareness inward to the core of your body, the area that includes your throat, heart area, stomach, and abdomen. After a bit, see if you get a subtle feeling-sense that would be difficult to put into words—as if the whole of your life were contained in this vague, indefinable feeling. It might be a pleasant feeling, or unpleasant, or merely neutral—whatever it is, simply notice that you're able to sense it somehow. Even if you think you're feeling "nothing," just notice that.

And now bring your awareness back into the room.

This is something you can do whenever you think of it—pause for a moment and sense inwardly, being curious to discover what's there. You might not get down to the sense of your core wound quite yet, but it's a start.

Learning to trust the intelligence of Being

There is much more to divinely human awakening than simply experiencing your core wound. When you begin to let up on the reins of control that you've been using your whole life, when you begin to let the horse that is your life-force have its head a little, you will make some discoveries about life that you might have been overlooking in your zeal to be in charge.

We could say that "Being" is life itself, the aliveness that quite magically transforms ephemeral spirit into tangible matter, and then gives sentience to that matter so it can delight in its creative expression. Being is vastly intelligent, and holds the templates for the evolutionary unfolding of all life. It also holds the template for *your* life's unfoldment into its full and total potential.

Just as your body naturally maintains its life through its vast instinctive intelligence—with your heart beating rhythmically, your lungs expanding and collapsing, and a million processes going on simultaneously to maintain life—so too are you held and supported by a vast Intelligence that knows how to awaken you fully into your divinely human potential. You don't have to figure this all out—any more than you have to tell your heart to beat. And because awakening takes you beyond what you currently know from experience, you cannot use familiar modes of reasoning to get you there.

So, you can let yourself relax a bit. Ease off the reins, and consider the possibility that your horse knows its way to the best pastures, to use an analogy, and is going to take you there even if you take a nap in the saddle.

Relaxing in this way doesn't mean inaction, or stagnation. It just makes it easier to begin noticing what happens when you stop trying to manipulate your life from your ideas about how it ought to be. Your horse is a genius, in case you didn't know, and she's been waiting for a chance to show what she's capable of.

In the next chapter, you'll see how to go beyond merely relaxing and begin to actively *greenlight* your humanness in a way that most optimally supports your full unfoldment. But before we go there, a final note about relaxing. When you learn how you've been driving yourself to the brink through trying to control life, and when you're given a context that an alternative is possible, you can begin to ease off, relax, and trust a little that maybe things can work out all by themselves. This is a first step.

There are further degrees of relaxation that you will be encountering. Embodied awakening itself happens after you fully and finally stop resisting and let go into just being as you are, making room for your Conscious nature to fully inhabit and be here. You cannot force this because, of course, forcing is not relaxing. It happens when all the conditions are ripe for it, and the timing is by grace.

And although the primary shift, or divinely human awakening, happens in conjunction with a fundamental, core relaxation, by itself it does not immediately undo all the other automatic ways of being that you adopted in order to survive being here in a body. That actually comes later, as you integrate that awakening more and more fully into who you are. Your conditioning will fall away as Being grows stronger in you. You will become more and more relaxed in yourself and in your life, and this is one of the real fruits of awakening: a much greater level of ease and grace will fill your days, as you trust that the divine in you, as you, will carry and support you through whatever comes your way.

But first steps first.

4

GREENLIGHTING

Our Story: *As we relaxed out of trying to be the way we thought we "should" be, we began to honestly see and "greenlight" ourselves as we are in order to further our embodiment. We said yes to our total Being, permitting ourselves to show up however we were being in the moment.*

Much deeper than mere "acceptance," greenlighting does not mean complacency or resignation. Instead, it is an active curiosity, an ongoing inquiry that leads to deeper understanding and whole-being integration.

The power of loving what is

Consider this: you can't fully control thoughts and impulses.

There is a widespread idea that we can control our destiny by controlling our thoughts and/or the beliefs that underlie them. Sometimes the message is overt: think and grow rich! And sometimes the message is subtle, as in "Whatever were you *thinking* (that made you do that stupid thing)?" Although the intention of most positive-thinking teachings is to help empower people to be successful in their lives, there is a hidden shadow side to this framework that can be insidious.

In reality, you cannot fully control the thoughts you have, at least not directly. Thoughts are mysterious! Some are echoes of what you've ingested from media—from news, advertising, TV programming, music, movies, books, etc. Some are echoes of things your parents, teachers, bosses, and peers have said to you over time, both positive and negative. Some are repetitions of conclusions and decisions you made (beliefs) about yourself and the world in response to the situations and events you encountered.

Some of your thoughts and impulses will be positive and optimistic, some fearful and pessimistic, some judgmental and critical, some angry and reactive, some creative and playful, some sad and/or dissatisfied with life. Sometimes you will feel healthy, energized, and ready for whatever life brings. And sometimes you will be feeling anything but that, and simply want to crawl into a hole. Not only do you have a vast array of thoughts, and the feelings that correlate with those thoughts, you also have feelings about your feelings. You probably think it is only natural to like how you feel when you are "up" and to dislike how you feel when you are "down."

The blame game

Because we have the ability to reflect on our internal states of being, and because we are hard-wired to try to figure out what causes us to feel as we do in order to prevent a recurrence of unpleasant feelings (as well as to create more instances of "good" feelings), we tend naturally toward assigning blame for our feelings onto *something*. Commonly, that something will be a person or situation in our lives that appears to be blocking our happiness. It may be something in the present, or an incident from the past that, in our judgment, left us permanently damaged and unable to be happy now.

Problems occur when you eventually get tied up in knots of your own making. There is no longer such a thing as simply feeling whatever you're feeling: the thought or feeling now has a whole story around it, plus some ideas about how to change it— either to have more of a good feeling or to get rid of an uncomfortable one. You might feel overly responsible for all the thoughts and emotions that you have, and the result is embarrassment or shame when you are unable to deliver the idealized life experience you've been taught to desire.

But it doesn't have to be this way. In the last chapter, we spoke of relaxing out of your conditioned way of being, as you tire of trying to make your life work through your own efforts. The next step beyond relaxing is to begin actively *greenlighting* yourself, including all of your thoughts, feelings, impulses, and beliefs about reality.

Greenlighting is not passive resignation

"Greenlighting" is a term borrowed from the film industry. When a producer decides a script is basically good enough to take it into production, they say they are greenlighting the project. It means the project will go forward. It doesn't mean it's a final product yet—indeed, it may go through a whole series of rewrites and improvements along the way. But greenlighting means it is fundamentally okay and worthy of further development.

In a similar fashion, we can greenlight ourselves in our fundamental okay-ness and worthiness. Greenlighting is a powerful tool to help counteract all the programming we've internalized in our lives that tells us that we are NOT okay or worthy. It's not about passively resigning ourselves to how things are. Instead, greenlighting is based on the framework that we, like that film script, are a work in progress.

Greenlighting is not an affirmation

Affirmations and positive thinking practices attempt to assert the "truth" of something that is not currently apparent. For example, "I am showered with financial abundance," or "I am totally healthy." While this may have some value, the limitation of affirmations is that no matter how many hundreds of times you say or write such a statement, the conditioned part of you that holds a different view will not be displaced and will tend to reject the affirmation as wrong or untrue. It simply doesn't work to try to stuff feelings or paper over them with a false positivity. What is ignored, or not felt, will remain the same—it will keep coming back, over and over.

With greenlighting, we permit ourselves to think and feel as we do *without trying to change those thoughts or feelings*, or replace them with a different idea. We radically embrace what is with compassion, and then experience how it naturally moves toward greater wholeness.

Greenlighting is an active investigation

You are greenlighting when you actively permit exactly what's happening in you now—all of your faults, failings, and shortcomings as well as your gifts and strengths—in a spirit of curiosity about what can be discovered. Perhaps you feel ashamed of not living up to your ideals, or not being as good a person as you aspire to be. Perhaps you've hurt others, been dishonest, or committed something you (or your family, community, or church) considers wrong or a "sin." As you greenlight the resulting discomfort, you also greenlight the shame itself—meaning you allow yourself to feel it so you can learn more about what's going on. When you embrace whatever you're feeling, you can begin to investigate it in a way that begins to restore your natural wellness of being.

If you've been taught that you're responsible for your thoughts, feelings, and life experiences, you may harshly blame yourself for what you judge to be your weaknesses, limitations, and failures. You will also tend to blame yourself for your lack of success, or your lack of perfection. Self-blame leads to shame, and feelings of shame keep most of us in deep hiding, from one another and from ourselves.

We think of this as only normal. In our daily interactions, we put on a smile and pretend to be upbeat. We speak only of the things that we are proud of, and edit our story to avoid talking about the places where we feel less than successful, or the ways in which we are unhappy. We tell ourselves that we don't want to make anyone else uncomfortable, but what are we actually doing? We are presenting a false picture of being someone who has his or her act together. And as a consequence, most people go around thinking that everyone else has better lives, are more successful, and are happier than they really are. In our innate tendency to compare, we find ourselves lacking. This leads, in turn, to an even greater sense of shame and a greater impulse to lie to keep others from finding out.

Subtle hypocrisy

Many spiritual organizations foster an especially insidious type of hypocrisy when they outline a blueprint for acting, for example, as a "good Christian," or a "good Buddhist," or a "good New Thought (or New Age) Practitioner." Perhaps the ideal is described as someone who is always even-tempered, generous, upbeat, and never agitated. When there is a value scale around desirable and undesirable emotions, people begin to imitate the desired feelings when others are watching in order to be accepted, and hypocrisy is born. They say the "right" things and perhaps do the "right" actions, but it doesn't come from genuine spiritual awareness on their part—merely from trying to follow "the rules." The downside of this shows up when there is no tolerance for being a real, live human being who feels and thinks things that aren't in line with the prescribed dogma. Feeling this judgment can increase the desire to avoid letting others see you as you are, and increase your sense of being different or not fitting in. This can, in turn, lead to more shame, or, ironically, more arrogance, or both.

This need to project an image of being happy and successful is especially pronounced in those who take on the role of teachers, ministers, spiritual leaders, or advisors. After all, don't you want those you look to for advice to be accomplished at what they are teaching? If they are teaching about success, their lives must be the epitome of success, and if they are teaching about inner peace, they better not ever be agitated! This kind of expectation can become a prison to such a teacher or a leader, preventing them from being authentic in their expression. And it can perpetuate, for the student, a myth of false perfection that they strive (and inevitably fail) to emulate.

The saga of love, hate, and fear

We have been told by some of our greatest spiritual teachers that we should choose love over fear, that love can conquer all, heal all wounds, and make the world a better place. We have been led to believe that fear is undesirable; that it is the opposite of love and that it prevents us from realizing our dreams and potentials. It is easy to hate fear. And in a similar fashion, we are told that hatred is also the opposite of love, and that it prevents real brotherhood from arising. It is easy to hate hatred, and to want it to disappear from our world. But is this the best way to look at our human tendencies?

What is the deeper truth here? Isn't it obvious that love is more desirable than fear? Isn't it obvious that fearful people are more selfish and also more prone to create armies and weapons and even wage war? Wouldn't the world be better if we could stop reacting from anger, hatred, and paranoia? Wouldn't we feel better inside, too?

Let's take this apart carefully. When you hate and try to get rid of any part of what you are, you are being violent towards yourself, and this inner-directed violence contributes to outer-directed violence. You try to exert violent (as in forceful) control over yourself and then expect others to do the same with themselves—or you offer to do it for them. But what does this actually accomplish? We have not succeeded in eradicating fear, anger, or grief by these methods. They are too intrinsic to our nature to be eliminated. Instead, we've driven these emotions underground where they fester, only to blow up unpredictably and with high blast velocity due to the repressed energy suddenly being released.

You have an inherent survival mechanism that is on the alert for threats, and responds with fight, flight, and freeze signals that you feel as anger or fear. And even though you might rightly see the horrific violence that can result from the unrestrained actions of people motivated by these emotions, the very place where love can begin to grow is in the radical embrace of your survival-based feelings, thoughts, and emotions. They have an important function. You simply cannot eliminate your survival mechanism—it is essential to the continuation of the body-mind and hence, to all of your spiritual growth as well.

What you can do is learn to attend to *all* of your feelings with patience and compassion, and learn to value the messages they bring. When brought into the light of Presence and integrated into your whole being, they become allies, bringing you wise counsel. I'll talk more about how to do this in Chapter 5.

It's not easy being human

As members of a spiritual community or religious congregation we may go along with their hypocrisy in part because we want to believe there is a way for our lives to work out and for everyone to find happiness and peace. We want to believe that a better world than the one we live in is possible or at least that there is a way to find peace in the midst of the craziness. We want to think that there are authorities we can turn to who know more than we do and can show us the way. Many of us want others to tell us how to live our lives, because down deep we feel quite lost. We want our teachers and leaders to be paragons of virtue and success. And when they fall from grace, which they will sooner or later because NO ONE has a perfect life, we find ourselves deeply disappointed and disillusioned.

The inescapable truth is it's hard to be here. It's hard to be a human being. It's hard to live in this bewildering world where there is so much competition, chaos, and unpredictability. It is hard to live with all the impulses vying for our attention, and with the clamor of our thoughts judging, criticizing, and second-guessing our every move and feeling state. It's hard to experience the pressure we feel to get our lives in order, to be successful, and to be happy. Not to mention the pressure to take care of our children, our parents, our jobs, and our partners, and help *them* find happiness. And on top of all that, we're supposed to love every-one—when we haven't even learned how to be genuinely kind to ourselves. In this scenario, happiness is almost guaranteed to be out of reach!

You're not responsible for your past

Consider this: you didn't consciously choose to think the way you do, to draw the conclusions you have about life, or to have the particular set of gifts and limitations you have. You didn't consciously choose to be beautiful or plain, tall or short, male or female. You didn't consciously choose many of the traumas life brought you, or to have to re-experience those traumas every time a life situation reminds you of them. You didn't invent your conditioning—it just happened because you were a fairly blank slate that was inherently highly impressionable and easily influenced.

Even if you believe the opposite, that you chose your parents and your gender and the body you would have, and even the events that happened to you, in order to learn certain things about life, that doesn't mean that you are somehow guilty, or at fault for generating the painful parts of your life to date. The *kindest* way to be with yourself is to consider that how you got to be the way you are happened quite automatically due to the intersection of your unique genetic tendencies and the environment you found yourself in. You are how you are because you are. *You are not to blame.* In some mysterious way, you could not be other than you are—a mixture of abilities and limitations that gives you an utterly unique perspective on life that is colored by all that you are and all that you have encountered.

Greenlighting ego

Another reason you might be prone to self-loathing is due to spiritual teachings that caution about something harmful and destructive within, that you have to get rid of somehow. That something is commonly (and over-simplistically) called "the ego"—the part of you that considers itself an individual, separate from other individuals and in need of defending itself from outside threats. The ego's instincts for self-preservation are sometimes said to be the root of all evil.

These teaching go on to say that the only way you can achieve peace is to "kill the ego." And they thus set you up to distrust yourself, to fear that there is something insidious operating within you that you need to turn against and cast out in order to be okay, or good, or worthy of grace. But the ego is a necessary part of being human! It learns through experience and holds patterns of energy, thought, and emotion that enable you to quickly recognize and avoid danger and also navigate in complex social environments. It's true that egoic reactions can sometimes be extreme or inappropriate, but you would not survive long without the inborn self-protection mechanisms of the ego. Because the ego is the first line of self-preservation, it will do everything it can to avoid its own destruction. Killing the ego would be suicide!

I am not saying that it isn't useful to study and address the challenges created by ego. If you are overly-focused on self-defense, your relationships, which are nourished by openness and trust, suffer. There needs to be a balance between self-interest and the kind of openness and vulnerable sharing that promotes intimacy and allows love. There are other ways to support open-heartedness without violently attempting to remove intrinsic aspects of yourself.

Resisting and fighting a part of your own nature only serves to perpetuate internal splits, and leads to self-loathing. You are not likely to get to genuine self-love through this route. What if, instead, you were to greenlight the ego in all of its expressions of self-interest, fear, and distrust, and actually appreciate how those impulses help to keep you alive? Without survival, there can't very well be awakening!

What's more, it is not necessary to rid yourself of ego in order to awaken to your true and total nature. Once again: it is not necessary to eliminate egoic patterns in order to awaken. In the past, it was assumed that Spirit could not come fully alive unless the ego were nearly eradicated first, but as we are making a more detailed study of what actually happens in the awakening process, we are discovering that it's just not so. Spirit comes alive and awake right alongside our self-interest and even pettiness, and then begins to soften and transform our humanness so that it supports an ever-greater expression of our divinely human potential.

The good news is that the arising of greater Presence brings a new influence to bear on how the ego is structured and how it operates. The more we relax, and the more we greenlight, the more trust in Being grows. And with greater trust in Being, the ego begins to let down its guard a little, and its rough edges begin to get rubbed off. Once ego no longer feels solely responsible for our survival, and sees that there is something far bigger than its narrow self-sense operating to help with that, it gets to relax. Not go away entirely, because it is part of what keeps us alive, creates our personality, and helps us interface with the world around us. But much of what it thought it needed to do begins to dissipate.

Your story matters—because YOU matter

A corollary of ego is your personal story. Some teachings would have you believe that your personal story is only an exaggerated "drama," and that you should not indulge yourself in thinking that it matters. But it does matter because *you* matter! Your unique expression and history are utterly unrepeated anywhere, and it is precious. So many of us have been conditioned to feel embarrassed about our personal story, about the drama that is our life, but I would like to encourage you to reframe that. Sure, it is worth considering that you have selective memory, and that you have a particular interpretation of the events of your life that might be perpetuating some pain. But as we study the way the body stores traumas, we are learning that trauma patterns are deeply embedded. They are not merely thoughts that can be summarily banished, nor can the feelings they engender be bypassed by treating them as if they were somehow imaginary or unreal. If you have a body, you have a history that is recorded in the very energy matrix that is interwoven with your body.

The most effective and humane way to respond to being a human with a past is to take it seriously, and to bring loving attention to the places where the trauma patterns keep getting triggered, in order to help them heal into wholeness and freedom. We'll talk more about this in the next chapter, *Inseeing*.

Compassion for yourself as you are learning

Greenlighting applies to all of our thoughts, feelings, emotions, and reactions. Yes, even self-hatred or resisting greenlighting. Greenlighting includes the ways we resist and fight against how things are, and all the ways we automatically judge things. It may seem a little strange at first, but if you think in terms of giving friendly, curious attention to the thoughts and attitudes showing up within you—including feelings that are anything BUT friendly—you'll be on the right track.

Try this: three special words

Here's a simple step you can take right now. Whenever you feel an uncomfortable feeling, say to yourself, "something in me is feeling _____ (fill in the blank)." When you use these three magic words, "something in me," you are shifting your perspective from small to large. You are taking one step back from the emotion and getting bigger than it is.

Example: "I'm sad" becomes "something in me is sad."

Example: "I'm so upset" becomes "something in me is so upset."

Give it a try with some difficult or uncomfortable emotion that you're feeling or have felt recently. Can you sense the difference?

When you say "something in me" you are not trying to change or push away any feeling. You are simply bringing the more spacious aspect of who you are into the picture, that part of you that has room for whatever is arising and can welcome it.

Being bigger leads to compassion, and compassion leads to natural, unforced healing and forward movement.

As you allow yourself to feel whatever the feeling is, you can also let your hand move gently to the place in your body that feels upset. In this way, you begin to give friendly, soothing contact to that something in you that feels uncomfortable or distressed, making space for it to be as it is.

Greenlighting impulses too—and the sensual delight of being alive

Greenlighting also applies to impulses—those prompts you feel from deep within. When you greenlight your life-affirming impulses, you begin freeing up parts of yourself that have been long-suppressed, perhaps from your earliest days, to come more alive and express your true nature. As you begin to experiment with saying "yes" to your impulses, you will make many discoveries about who you are and what really matters to you in life.

Get into the sensual delight of being alive! Allow yourself to explore what actually feels good to your body and spirit. This could mean breathing fresh air and feeling the sun on your skin, or moving your body in dynamic ways like exercise, sports, yoga, qigong, etc. It could mean receiving more touch, from loved ones, or from massage or other bodywork. It can mean eating delicious things—simply giving yourself permission to follow some of those impulses you have to do things that *feel great*. And of course, your sexuality is one of those things that you might want to greenlight.

In all cases, I'm not suggesting you do things that would be harmful to yourself or others, or to your existing relationships. But for many people on a path of spiritual discipline, or even on rigorous programs of self-development, there's been way too much emphasis on austerity and denial of impulses. As you begin to awaken, it is through allowing yourself to experiment with what feels wonderful that you will rediscover your true nature. You may have forgotten how to be spontaneous in your quest to always do the "right" thing. So, consider giving yourself a vacation from that sort of self-control, and try some improvisation. Your body will thank you for it. It's much easier to come alive in a body that is content and experiences pleasure. There is more than enough pain in life; we need to also have pleasure and joy to counterbalance that and make life worth fully encountering.

I am not advocating that your life become all about hedonism. Ultimately I'm inviting that which is deepest and truest in you to come fully alive and find expression here. As you are experimenting, stay in touch with the feedback you get, with how your body feels afterward. Did that really satisfy something, or not? Underneath a more obvious urge (like eating a pint of ice cream), there might be a deeper, more significant impulse that would be important to discover. Perhaps you are longing for a deeper connection with someone? Or maybe you're frustrated in your job and need to find opportunities for greater self-expression?

If you've been turning down too many of your impulses, you might also be missing some important clues about what will move your life forward in the most auspicious ways.

Can greenlighting go too far?

What I've been saying may be triggering some concerns and fears. Am I advocating that you greenlight ALL your impulses, including those that are destructive or that hurt others?

First, let me make a distinction between impulses and actions. An impulse is an urge, a prompt from somewhere inside you, and yes, I do recommend greenlighting all the impulses, thoughts, and feelings that arise in you. By greenlighting, you show yourself compassion for how you are predisposed to think and feel in certain patterns. But as far as *acting out* your impulses, that's a different story. I strongly advocate acting only upon impulses that feel life-affirming, for you and for any others who might be affected. Of course, you would *not* be advised to act on an impulse to do violence to another person (except in the extreme case where you or your loved ones are in imminent danger). Nor should you encourage another to act out those sorts of impulses.

If for any reason you are having trouble with basic levels of impulse control, or find yourself too often giving in to impulses that are socially disruptive, please find a good therapist to work with to help you gain a level of mastery. You will need a good foundation to build upon as you progress through the many steps of your awakening process.

Greenlighting the world

You are the way you are because you are, and, in a similar fashion, the world is as it is because it is. There is something about the structure of the world that generates the balance required to maintain life—the balance of life and death, of growth, sustenance, and destruction.

We can observe the net perfection that maintains homeostasis on earth all around us. Life is continually adapting and renewing itself. The whole ecosystem of the earth has been likened to a body, with a natural system for rebalancing. Our earth is amazingly intelligent and resourceful at maintaining herself, much as our bodies do a great job of maintaining their health, given half a chance. This is not to make light of the ecological crisis currently stressing the planet, for it is possible that the earth has never been faced with this kind of a predicament in the past. We do indeed need to take deliberate action to support the restoration of the natural balance—to give the earth enough support so she can shake off the many serious challenges that are threatening the continuation of life as we know it.

Just as each person experiences a core wound when they contrast their sense of possibility against their very finite limits, so too do we often suffer from the painful limits we see in the world around us, because we compare them against our idealized sense of how we think the world should be. It's heartbreaking, as well as bewildering, to witness senseless destruction, horrendous violence, wars, genocide, starvation, oblivious disregard for the environment, and so on. It's no wonder we find it painful, and want it to change.

If you're mostly focusing on what's wrong, you might feel panicky about the state of the world and have a hard time greenlighting it, seeing primarily the many problems, inequities, and ways that things appear to be veering dangerously out of balance. But much as greenlighting our personal thoughts and feelings gives us a better opportunity to look at them and help them move toward greater wholeness, greenlighting the world can be a first step toward understanding and cooperating with her natural healing processes.

The alternative is to be at war with how things are—to be continually noticing only what you don't like or approve of, or to be judging what you observe as if you could do a better job if you were made king or queen of the universe. Many people operate as if the way to make things work is to hate all those things that they don't agree with, in some misguided attempt to coerce others (or themselves) to comply with whatever arbitrary standard or ideal that they hold. But in the long run, what is accomplished? There is more hatred in the world, and the cult of dissatisfaction simply gains another disciple.

But what if we were to greenlight the world as well as ourselves? We could stop blaming anyone or anything including God (however you define "God") for how things are. We could remind ourselves that things simply are as they are, and that life has managed to continue so far. And from that open-hearted place, we could begin to envision how we might become better shepherds of life so that its systems work even more successfully. We do not have to hate how things are in order to care for them and support their fullest unfolding.

A balance of freedom and limits

In practical terms, the setup here includes both freedom (potentials) and limits (specific conditions). Every situation in life contains elements of both—if the situation leans strongly toward one end or the other, it will sooner or later be swinging back to the other polarity. It cannot be other than this given the nature of the world.

Once I fully got this—deeply understood this and began applying it to all the situations of my life—I relaxed into life much more deeply than ever before. The idea that I could experience only the parts of life I wanted and exclude the rest was revealed to be a myth that I was holding onto, a myth that caused me a lot of discontent. It was only when I surrendered to the inevitable limits that I became able to open myself to the potentials that were also present in every situation. Greenlighting life, far from being a resignation to "how things are," unleashed me to explore possibilities as never before, not from fear of terrible consequences if I failed to control things according to my ideas of right and wrong, but out of love for life, love for my fellow humans, and love for the earth herself.

Unleashing the power of greenlighting

Remember that greenlighting does not mean passive complacency, but is a generous attitude of accepting how things are in the moment with an eye to how they can evolve most auspiciously in the future. Most of us have not experienced much greenlighting, and we will need to have it modeled for us in order to learn how to do it. Being told is not enough. And it does not happen overnight.

This is why the biblical injunction to "love your neighbor as yourself" is so difficult to follow. Sure, you might *intend* to be loving, but if you've experienced many demands, expectations, and criticisms from others, you might not have an inner template of how to do that. Being loving means to be kind, and to be kind begins with greenlighting. Another way of saying this is to *hold ourselves and one another blameless for what has happened in the past*, while actively exploring why we feel and react as we do. Then we can help one another relax and grow in the light of love, rather than in the toxic domain of judgment.

This is why it is immensely valuable to have association with awakened teachers and others who are learning to relate in this fashion. Teachers who have embodied greenlighting are able to provide a form of re-mothering—relating to us as we always wished our mothers would relate to us—and thereby provide what many of us never got enough of. They see and support our efforts without blaming us when we fall short of our ideals and goals. They gently remind us when we are being overly hard on ourselves or others, so that we can begin to relax our tight grip on our lives. They embody a sense of trust in the natural wisdom of Being that supports life and wholeness and helps us find our way. It is through templating on conscious, embodied teachers that we begin to be able to greenlight ourselves. This is the beginning step of self-love, which can eventually spread to love of our neighbors and our world.

It is not necessary to so despise your nature that you can no longer see the beautiful being that you are. That's heartbreaking! But how can you know otherwise, if that's what was modeled for you? The solution to this sorry state of affairs is to find and keep company with people who are learning a different way of being, and to absorb their healing energies and their loving kindness—to "tank up" on their greenlighting. And when you have absorbed enough, you will in turn become a source of that same healing energy for others.

Once you've begun to relax out of your old strategies for living, and have begun practicing greenlighting of yourself and the world as it is, you are ready to begin learning more about what makes you tick. In Chapter 5, I'll explore how the practice of *Inseeing* can help you discover the many aspects of who you are, and how to use the power of Presence to help you evolve most auspiciously.

5

INSEEING

Our Story: We became aware of the patterns of our conditioning that were once useful in supporting our survival but were now often seen to be unhealed "broken zones" keeping us separate, inauthentic, and unavailable for real intimacy and aliveness. We discovered how we could bring interested curiosity to our investigation of these conditioned "partial selves," and welcome them to be as they are without trying to fix or change them. Lo and behold, when given conscious attention, they began to organically move toward greater wholeness and freedom.

Recognizing how you're configured

There is tremendous value in learning how your inner territory operates, and the effects of your configuration on your life experience. Although you are not to blame for how you are wired, in this moment you can begin to be more aware of your patterns and conditioning. When you see your patterns in a conscious, compassionate way—when you *insee* them—they lose some of their ability to control your behavior. *Inseeing* is the art of bringing conscious awareness and Presence to your inner process so it can organically move toward healing and integration, thus providing you greater freedom to act in ways that truly serve your best interests in the moment.

Most of your attitudes and patterns were formed in the past in response to your life circumstances and events. They represent *who you have been*. They are not your total self. Although your total self does include the conditioned aspects of your personality, you are always more than that, more than the sum of your parts, more than the limitations of your temperament. However, you might be experiencing some undue distress from unhealed, frozen aspects of your total self that are still viewing life from the perspective of, for example, a two-year old. The process of *Inseeing*, which will be explained later in this chapter, brings unconditional Presence to such parts in order to help them evolve toward greater wholeness—by helping them get current with who you are now as an adult.

Unseen patterns drive us unconsciously

The way most of us behave most of the time is quite automatic (even if we like to think we are acting from our own free will). The experiences of our early life left tracks in our psyche, and energy runs through these existing tracks more easily than it does in novel ways. Therefore, when we encounter a situation that reminds us of situations in the past (whether we consciously make the connection or not), our bio-computer overlays the template from the past onto the present and causes us to operate in pre- determined ways.

For example: Sue was raised in a home with an alcoholic mother who would at times fly off the handle and strike whichever child caught her attention. Sue learned that the best thing to do, at the first sign of anger or disapproval from her mother, was to get very still and quiet—in effect, to freeze up. Now as an adult, Sue works in a business setting with a boss who at times gets frustrated and angry. Although her boss never acts it out physically, Sue recognizes her boss's clenched jaw as a sign of danger, and she freezes up in response, sometimes even trembling, and is unable to continue her work.

These conditioned reaction patterns lie below the threshold of your conscious awareness, like a shadow, waiting for the right combination of input to become activated. When they flare up, seemingly out of nowhere, you might find yourself saying, "I don't know what came over me; I just wasn't myself."

Broken zones

A pattern of extreme reaction to a fairly innocent situation is a *broken zone*. Broken zones are places in our psyches that were wounded by traumatic events, and subsequently become hyper-sensitive and hyper-vigilant about anything resembling the original wounding. Broken zones always link to some event in the past, when we were unable to avoid being hurt. If we were unable to fully experience that event at the time, due to lack of support, being too young to process it fully, or due to the sheer intensity of the experience, some of the shock becomes embedded in our energetic matrix. When life brings us a situation that reminds us of that trauma, it is like hitting a raw nerve with a dentist's drill: our reaction can be far greater than the situation seems to warrant. We may lash out in anger, collapse in sorrow, freeze into immobility, or engage in distracting behaviors to override or numb the uncomfortable feelings.

Everyone has broken zones. They are very challenging to deal with because they remain hidden from us and others until someone stumbles over them. Then—voila—there they are, full blown and distrusting everyone and everything around them. When you are triggered in this fashion, it may seem impossible to do anything but helplessly watch as your emotions take control. However, by allowing yourself to feel the distress in your body more consciously, you will find that you can begin to explore the depth of the zone in a healing manner.

A broken zone is like a *partial self*, a repetitive reaction state that has an attitude, or an agenda, but doesn't have the whole picture of your life as it is now. (The term "partial self" and the definition here is from the Treasure Maps to the Soul work of

Barbara McGavin and Ann Weiser Cornell.) *Inseeing* is more than simply an intellectual or emotional process: it uses the inherent wisdom of the body to gain important insights about the original injury and the decisions you made about life at that time. Over time (and with some skillful help) more of the trauma will be released, thus lessening the impact of the wound on your life now.

It's important to understand that broken zones are formed by your instinct for survival and their existence is not a sign that you have done anything wrong. The problem with broken zones is that they interfere with living a spontaneous, joyful existence. By the time you have reached midlife, you may have accumulated so many prickly spots that you're all too frequently reacting to perceived threats. And when you're reacting, you are not really able to evaluate the situation as it actually is, or to be present with the people around you (much less to be intimate with them, because intimacy requires a sufficient degree of trust and relaxation to let other people in).

To recap: automatic reaction patterns have helped you to stay safe. While they may occasionally perform a similar function in your current life, they also interfere with your ability to be present and creatively respond to the situations and people you are encountering *now*. They interfere with your ability to be intimate, for whenever you perceive your loved ones through a lens that says they are a threat to you, you will shut down in an attempt to keep yourself safe. Most fundamentally, they rob you of freedom and satisfaction in life.

This dynamic, the threat-recognition-and-reaction patterning, is sometimes referred to as *ego*. And because it does interfere with your ability to be present and responsive in your current life, it is labeled as "bad," and some spiritual teachers tell you that you should get rid of it (as if "it" was a single thing that could somehow be excised out of you).

But this patterning is extremely resistant to being removed, and for good reason. It actually *does* contribute to your survival. Removing it would be like removing the anti-virus software from your computer. Sure, your programs might boot up faster, and you wouldn't have to deal with those warning messages, but you would lose some essential safeguards. It would be foolish to remove the entire programming.

Broken zones won't prevent your awakening

The existence of your conditioned response patterns is not inherently wrong or bad, nor is it something that has to be eliminated in order to awaken to your divinely human nature.

That's worth repeating: your conditioned response patterns—your ego, your broken zones, your shadow—are not inherently wrong or bad, and they do not need to be eliminated in order for you to awaken into your divinely human potential. They are *part* of you, and no less divine than any other aspect of what makes you tick.

However, though conditioning does not prevent a divinely human awakening, when it is especially strong, neurotic, or obsessive, it can keep your attention so bound up in circular thinking or strong emotions that it gets in the way of doing the inquiry needed to clarify Consciousness (we'll get into this more in the chapter on awakening). Learning to observe and be with your patterning in a conscious way will make it easier to focus on awakening, and enhance the quality of your life as well.

Freeing up energy and attention

It is possible to bring a new level of understanding to these processes and thus free up energy and attention from the places it has been bound. In effect, you begin writing new code so that your bio-computer stops perceiving so many things as threats and has more energy for creativity. More and more, your essential self will be free to express itself in this life, and the freer you are, the more room or space there will be for your infinite divine nature to come alive and fully awaken.

About now you might be wondering, "Can we ever be completely free of these patterns? Can these broken zones be healed for good?" The answer to that is a qualified "yes." You can encounter a pattern so fully, and feel it all the way to the very bottom, so that it completely unwinds itself and no longer shows up in response to any circumstances. More typically, however, a pattern will continue to exist as part of your programming, but when the energy or force that was bound up in it dissipates, it no longer drives your behavior. It's somewhat like letting the air out of a balloon. It is still a balloon, but if you prick it it's not going to explode.

You might also be wondering, "Is it necessary to go into therapy and re-experience all your past traumas in order to get free of this baggage?" Well, it depends. What it depends on is the nature and severity of the wounding you have incurred. While we all have broken zones, some of us received trauma so extreme that we got severely set back, and never learned some of the essential skills of human relating—such as being able to trust others.

For example, a person who was molested by someone they thought was safe may have lost ability to trust to such a degree that they now find themselves living an isolated existence, unable to feel relaxed and open with others. They have not learned how to distinguish real danger from more subtle threats, nor to distinguish whether someone's loving approach is truly benign or has a violent agenda of sexual conquest. This degree of injury calls for extra support from very skillful helpers who can provide the steady safety and understanding that will lead to real and lasting healing.

The good news is that even people with severe traumas or neuroses can and do awaken to their divinely human nature. It is not necessary to undertake an exhaustive project of "fixing" oneself in order to awaken.

However, fulfilling the potential of such an awakening *will* require bringing conscious attention to the unconscious, or automatic, ways you behave, so that you can more fully express the awakening you've had. Embodied awakening is typically accompanied by a raw, unbuffered revisitation of painful limits and broken zones, and this encounter can be quite stark and challenging. Fortunately, there is an intelligence of Being that, in most cases, will protect you from the intensification that comes with awakening until your personality has enough resilience to handle the influx of higher frequencies. The awakened spirit itself then begins modifying your configurations—in a sense "rewriting your code"—so that you become ever-more able to live and express that awakened spirit.

Whether before or after your divinely human awakening, and whether or not you feel that you have some severe psychological issues to deal with, it is highly desirable that you begin to study how your inner world operates so that you can befriend it and use it in an optimal way, rather than being at its mercy.

Body wisdom

Before I get into the specifics of how Inseeing works to create deep and lasting healing and wholeness, I want to introduce something that is very core to the entire project of *embodied* awakening, which is what we're exploring here. The project is to become divinely human, rather than automatons whose personalities got formed early in life and then continued to operate on auto-pilot. It's about taking the divine spark that lies fairly dormant in the hearts of all people and providing it with the right mixture of fuel and air so that it can flame into a life of creative expression.

At the very heart of this awakening process is the body. Not only the physical body (which many spiritual teachings say is at the other end of the spectrum from spirit), but the entire subtle energetic matrix of the body—that intelligent field that knows all about how to support life, growth, and healing, and holds the template for your most auspicious unfoldment in this life. Some call this total matrix the unconscious or subconscious, some call it Being, or, as I have somewhat humorously referred to it in this book, as the bio-computer whose programming we are seeking to upgrade for more optimal functioning. What's important is to understand that when I say *inner body*, I am referring to a highly intelligent system that is constantly at work supporting all the functions that maintain life and permit experience here as a human being. This inner body is the *other* aspect of what we are that isn't the thinking mind. It includes our emotions and intuitions plus all that is typically subconscious and hidden from view. This intelligence of the inner body can also be called *body wisdom*.

Due to the dominance of the thinking mind, most people perceive life primarily through their thoughts and mental evaluations. Although their bodies are also highly intelligent and constantly aware of everything they are encountering, most people have very limited awareness of what's going on in their bodies, or how tuning into the body's wisdom could really enhance their lives. The thinking mind has linear intelligence firing very quickly but it gives us only a small fraction of everything we could be aware of—a sort of Cliffs Notes version of the information that comes from our subconscious minds. On the other hand, the inner body has a more spherical intelligence which fires more slowly and is holistic, comprehensive, and rich with meaning. This body-consciousness, vaster than the linear mind, generates complex feeling states that can be used to access whole-being intelligence, once we reconnect the wiring that allows us to tap into it.

Many teachings point to our habit of identifying so strongly with our thinking minds as THE problem that keeps us from being able to awaken into our divinity. However, the proposed solution of trying to somehow stop the mind from operating has proven impossible for most people to achieve, leading them to feel that they are failures and that awakening is out of their reach.

Now, however, there is an entirely different way of addressing this challenge that is becoming available to more and more people as modern western psychology experiments with various forms of body-centered therapies. One of the recent discoveries is that by *including* the inner body's wisdom, you can operate with much greater intelligence, empowerment, and freedom of choice, without needing to silence the mind. The surface mind can go right on with its surface, linear thinking, without unduly interfering with the operation of what we might call higher (embodied) consciousness.

It's ironic. For centuries we have been told by our elders and spiritual teachers that the body was merely the repository of baser impulses and instincts, and that we should not trust it. In order to be more spiritual, we should actively do our best to screen it out of our awareness so that we can be more "pure." But all along, our bodies have actually been the home of our greatest intelligence and also the very place where our divine spirit could come into harmony with all of our physical, emotional, and mental currents in order to bring our divine humanity to life. I invite you to test it out for yourself.

Learning to tune into and listen to the inner body's wisdom is not difficult, once you get a sense of the framework and why this approach is so valuable. You may need to practice for awhile with someone who is skilled in helping you attune to your body's communication and engage with it in a greenlighting manner. Once you get the hang of it, you will be able to do this on your own, or in partner relationship with others who are learning to use Inseeing in support of their own awakening process.

The Inseeing Process™

The process of Inseeing that I describe below is, in large part, based on the brilliant system of Inner Relationship Focusing developed by Ann Weiser Cornell and Barbara McGavin. "Inseeing" is a term used by the German poet Rilke to describe the experience of seeing into another living being so totally that it is as if you were standing in their center and understanding them from their own perspective. You *insee* their wholeness and divine perfection, in and of itself, without needing to change it in any way.

Not merely a means of experiencing others in a profound way, Inseeing is also a way of seeing into your own inner territory. As you enter into the various parts and come to understand them from within, their inherent perfection and wholeness is revealed. When you can be with your inner parts in this manner, then relaxing, greenlighting, and self-compassion will really come alive for you in a way that will accelerate your awakening. The process of exploring your inner territory through Inseeing can be divided into eight steps:

I Identify something to work with—an issue, a problem, or some distress you've been feeling

N Notice how it feels in your body—the felt sense of it

S Speak what it feels like, and double-check that the words you're using to describe it really fit

E Engage with it by saying hello or otherwise acknowledging that you're aware of it

E Invite it to express how it's feeling or what it wants (or doesn't want)

I Receive any insights and let it know you're hearing it

N See if it needs anything further from you right now— or wants you to do anything

G Express your gratitude for whatever came into your awareness

1) Identify

You identify something to explore when you notice that you are having a reaction, or are feeling concerned about something, or want to get more clarity about a situation in your life. There might be some emotion stirring, or perhaps you might notice that you are thinking obsessively, as if something has taken over your experience and there is some charge around it. The first step is to simply notice that something's going on, and to take some time to give it some greenlighting attention.

Inseeing typically begins with pausing and taking a few moments to get in touch with how your body is feeling right now. You might do this by noticing the feeling of contact with the chair you are sitting on, and then the feeling of contact between your feet and whatever they are resting on. Then you might tune into the feeling of your calves, your thighs, your hips, your back—

moving slowly through different parts and checking in with how they're feeling right now. Then your shoulders, arms, hands—perhaps sensing that subtle feeling in the palms of your hands. Then check into the back of your neck, your scalp, your forehead and cheeks. Now take a full breath and notice any feeling of enlivenment that comes with that.

By tuning into the sensations of your physical body, you are opening yourself to the complex sensations being generated by your inner body as it registers and reflects the *whole* of your life situation as it is in this moment. You are also bringing forward the quality of Presence: that aspect of your whole being that is able to bring warm, interested curiosity to whatever's arising.

2) Notice

Now begin to bring your attention inward, into the core of your body. Notice the feeling inside your throat, your chest, your stomach, and your belly. The core area of throat and torso is where it is typically easiest to get the ***felt sense*** of whatever's wanting your attention—although a felt sense can appear anywhere in (or sometimes near) your body.

"Felt sense" is a term from Eugene Gendlin, the noted American philosopher and psychotherapist who first defined felt sense and developed the process of Focusing. A felt sense is the freshly arising holistic sense of a complex situation. Your body is continually generating feelings that correspond to your thoughts and emotions. For example, that fluttery sensation in your gut when someone close to you says "we need to talk." Or perhaps your face flushes when you feel angry with someone. Or you feel a pain in the area of your heart when you think about a romantic relationship that went badly. There's an endless variety of such physical expressions of psycho-emotional issues.

Emotions themselves have familiar feelings, too: sadness is often heavy, while anger is pressing, and fear is contracting. Sometimes the felt sense will come as an image or a metaphor or a memory of some incident from the past. For instance, you might get a sense of a snake coiling around in your belly, or a sword thrust through your heart. These are all examples of how your inner body-wisdom communicates with your thinking mind when given the opportunity.

By allowing yourself to feel the issue somewhere in your body, you begin the process of connecting your thinking mind with your body and opening the lines of communication between them. This is important, because your body has a built-in healing mechanism, not only for the physical system but also for the psycho-emotional system. Eugene Gendlin, the founder of Focusing, said, "What is not seen and not felt remains the same, but what is seen and felt *moves.*" That is, it moves in the direction of healing and wholeness, or as he sometimes said, *fresh air.*

What's "not seen and not felt" are all those imprints we acquired throughout our lives from incidents that we felt hurt by, that lie below the threshold of awareness. They live in the subtle, cellular memory, waiting to be reactivated by some triggering stimulus. And as such, they will repeat over and over again, unchanging, unless they are brought into conscious awareness and *felt.* No amount of thinking has the power to create this type of deep healing and release of trauma. It is simply insufficient to the task. You might think you know all about what is happening and why, but find yourself continuing to feel and react the same way every time the situation arises, without any fundamental shift— until you bring it to a higher level of consciousness by *feeling it in the body* with full awareness.

We typically respond to these uncomfortable physical feelings by trying to screen them out of our awareness. This is only natural, since we were never taught how to listen to them in a way that would be healing and enlivening. Without that knowledge, to feel them is only to suffer them over and over, which almost no one would consciously choose to do. So instead we live with such things as frequent headaches, high blood pressure, back pain, or stomach aches. Our unheeded physical symptoms may well progress to ill-nesses, as our bodies shout louder and louder to get our attention.

Of course, ignoring our body's distress call is not the only cause of disease, but it is often one of the contributing factors.

3) Speak

At first, you may have only a vague, fuzzy, difficult-to-describe sense that somehow correlates with the whole situation you are exploring. This is normal. You notice that you're feeling *something* there. Your body's "thinking" happens at a slower pace than that of your mind—something like an image appearing out of fog—so it's important to stay with the vague feeling for a while, allowing it to become gradually clearer.

A felt sense can be strong and vivid, or it can be as subtle as a shy animal hiding in the bushes. However it appears, as it becomes more distinct, it is important to find a word, phrase, image, or metaphor that accurately represents what you are noticing—and speak it aloud. Say "I am sensing something in me that _____" or "I am noticing something that _____ (and fill in the blank)." This step helps make the link between your thinking mind and your body's wisdom. Try on a description, and as you are attending inwardly, you will notice that when you find *the right descriptor* something shifts slightly, as if your body is saying "yes, you got it!" to your thinking mind. If you don't get that sense of "yes," try again with another description until something clicks.

4) Engage

Once you've described it, the next thing to do is formally acknowledge it. It may seem strange to say hello to something that is, after all, a part of you, but this step helps to initiate an inner relationship with something in you that is trying to get your conscious attention. Before you can invite it to tell you more about itself, you need to make its acquaintance, so to speak. A good way to do this is to simply say hello. Or, if "hello" doesn't feel right, an alternative is to inwardly acknowledge it: "I see you there." This might feel uncomfortable if what's showing up is something you don't like about yourself, something you might rather ignore or tell to get lost, but that kind of treatment only leads to suppression, not to healing and growth. Acknowledging what is there is a very powerful step forward. If the issue at hand is amenable to your contact, you will feel some sort of a response to your greeting. It may brighten up, as if happy to be noticed, or the feeling of distress might become more acute. Whatever response comes, it is useful information and sets the stage for further investigation.

5) Express

Beyond feeling the issue as a physical sensation or an image or a metaphor, the next step of bringing it into full awareness is to hang out with it a bit and invite it to reveal what's going on. A *partial self* is an aspect of who you are, formed in the past, that doesn't yet have the whole picture. Maybe it's concerned or afraid about something in your current life, and wants to prevent something bad from happening. Or maybe it wants to generate something creative and new. You might begin by sensing into it as if you could see things from its perspective, or discern what emotion it's feeling. If you do sense a particular emotion, you might see if you get a sense of what's causing it to feel that way.

Or you might invite it to tell you what's going on with it. Rather than cross-examine it with direct questions, it's usually better to see if it *wants* to tell you what's up. Sometimes there will be a flood of information coming forth instantly, but other times there may be resistance to communicating and a need for greater trust to be developed first. Perhaps this one feels like it's been ignored so many times that it doesn't believe you will really listen, so it clams up. With a bit of patient attention from you, it might come around.

The important thing is to stay open and be respectful, letting it know you are interested and available to listen. Let whatever happens be okay. What brings healing forward movement is to warmly *be with* the issue, without trying to fix it, control it, reason with it, or make it go away. Greenlight it as it is, and make sure you really listen to what it has to say. Even if it is telling you off!

6) Insights

Be sure to acknowledge that you are receiving whatever this partial self is communicating. This can be as simple as repeating back what you heard, such as, "Yes, I hear that you _____ (fill in the blank). Would you like to tell me more?"

When you listen attentively to its concerns—when you GET it—this partial self can begin to relax. While partial selves don't have the whole picture, nevertheless their information is important for your wellbeing. If you don't listen to them, they tend to get agitated and send up louder and louder signals, because they are hard-wired for your survival. They can get panicky and try to run the show if they don't have anyone to report to, and they can become like horrible nags, or incessantly critical voices—until it's no wonder you think that they have nothing of value to offer you.

However, when you do listen to them (which does not mean blindly obeying, but rather listening respectfully to their input), they can transform into powerful allies. They very often feel satisfied that they have done their job and are now content to step back and let you—the whole-being you—take the necessary appropriate actions.

7) Needs

It's useful to see if this part needs or wants anything from you right now. There might be an action that it wants you to take— or not take. Or perhaps it would like a good-faith commitment from you to come and listen to it again soon, because it has more it wants to contribute.

Another way to invite creative input from a part is to ask it whether there is something it would enjoy. Whatever comes, be sure to acknowledge that you heard its request, and if it is something you're willing to do, let it know that.

8) Gratitude

The very important final step is to express your gratitude to whatever came. Let it know you are happy that it was willing to communicate, and that you will be open to future communication as well.

Try this: Inseeing

The next time you find yourself triggered by something, or feeling confused or upset, take a moment to pause and go within. Find a time when you can be alone and quiet. It's useful to have a notebook with you to record any insights that come.

Then go through the steps of the Inseeing Process in order, inviting whatever wants some attention to come forward as you listen closely to what it has to say. Find that place in you that is warm, patient, and curious to know more, and listen from there. Don't assume that you "already know what it's about." Stay open to what might be new about the situation in this moment, because you may get surprised by some aspect you hadn't heard before. Don't worry about doing this perfectly—your intention to be a good listener to yourself is more important than the technique you use.

Make a note of any insights, and be sure to express your appreciation for whatever came.

The x-factor: Presence

There is something in you that is spacious enough to welcome all the different feelings, emotions, reactions, fears, and judgments that arise in you without being overwhelmed by them. We could call this something *Presence*.

"Presence" is a term for something ineffable and difficult to grasp with the mind, but that is available to be noticed once you attune to it. Some might call it the Witness, and others might call it your soul or higher self. Whatever it is called, it is bigger than, and not limited by, the conditioned patterns of your mind and personality.

Ann Weiser Cornell, the originator of *Inner Relationship Focusing*, defines Presence as the state of being with whatever is in your awareness, and knowing that what you are with is *part* of you, not all of who you are. Presence is that aspect of your nature that can be aware of your behavior while not losing touch with it in a personal way. Presence includes all the patterns of your personality, both your winning strategies and your broken zones, but is also more than the sum of the parts. It is more than thoughts and emotions, as well. Presence can be aware of anything that's arising and can give it unconditional attention and warm curiosity. And it does that simply by acknowledging each quality or issue as it arises: "Oh, hello, I see you there."

Presence is a quality that is available to everyone at least in latent form. It is Presence that makes Inseeing such a powerful practice for deep healing and transformation. In Chapter 6, I will discuss ways to cultivate Presence so that it becomes a more active part of your life.

The importance of inner work to divinely human awakening

At this point you may be wondering if tuning into potentially painful or unpleasant feeling states is really necessary for awakening. Isn't enlightenment supposed to bring feelings of bliss, and freedom from suffering? And if you focus on unpleasant things, won't that bring more of them into your life?

In response to those questions, I want to remind you that we are speaking here about *embodied,* divinely human awakenings—those that include all of what it is to be a person without trying to deny, escape, avoid, or override our very human ways of thinking and reacting. Embodied awakening is not easy—no one said it would be. And it won't be easy, at first, to bring the repressed parts of your psyche into conscious view. We've all done and experienced things we'd rather forget, or things we feel ashamed of that we'd prefer to keep hidden from others—and hidden from ourselves, as well. But when we begin to allow these things to come to the attention of our conscious mind, where we can acknowledge them, and invite them to give us whatever gifts they have to offer, we liberate a powerful, natural process in us that moves the issue, and our lives, forward. Instead of remaining stuck in the tangled morass of our subconscious body-mind, the issue is brought into the fresh air of current reality where it can be transformed naturally and organically into something that can be a positive force in our lives. Our body-wisdom already knows how to do this, if we will follow the steps of Inseeing to cooperate with it rather than fighting against it.

Compassion

With greenlighting we acknowledge ourselves as we are—with our strengths, yes, but also with our weakness in the face of our conditioning and habits. No matter how much we might strive to be otherwise, we all at times act in automatic, unconscious ways that are sometimes hurtful to others, or ourselves. We begin to see how much of our life energy is caught up in obsessively thinking about our problems, issues, fears, and sorrows, or how we dwell on our regrets about the past and concerns about the future. We learn how it's impossible to avoid being conditioned in this way, and that it's not our fault—we are innocent in this process. We begin to see how difficult it is to be here as a human being, with such a strong intellect that leaves us feeling so cut off from our spiritual nature. As we begin to accept our humanness, we begin to relax.

Beyond greenlighting is the final step of compassion. Compassion cannot be forced, but it naturally begins to arise when we really get that we could not have prevented the way we were created or the ways we have acted in the past. Compassion arises when we see how caught up we often are in our fixed patterns of behavior, and how unkind we have been to judge ourselves—as well as others—so harshly. Compassion is a quality of Presence that spontaneously arises when we let go of our self-hatred and begin to feel kindly toward ourselves, willing to see how we are truly doing the best we can.

As compassion begins to arise in our relationship with our various inner parts, we discover that we do not need to push away *anything* that is in us. Everything reveals itself to have a positive intention for our lives, even if it seems at first to be an obstruction to forward movement. We don't have to force anything to change or be different, or give up its position. In the alchemy of deep listening, forward movement is the natural outcome, and it can show up in novel and surprising ways.

Learning the Inseeing Process

When first learning to use the Inseeing Process, it is most useful to have an Inseeing guide holding the space for you when you are investigating an issue. It is not enough to know, intellectually, that attending to your felt senses is a good idea, and that you should be patient with yourself in the process. If you have not had this type of behavior modeled for you (and most of us have not) it will probably be just another empty concept. In the learning stage, a skilled listener is essential, one who can model for you how to be with the various aspects that begin showing up once you have invited them, and how to gently sense into what they want or need from you. And a skillful guide will also demonstrate how to be compassionate with yourself when you are feeling ashamed, or when you can't greenlight something even though you wish you could.

Being with your inner process can get a bit complicated, which is another reason for enrolling a skilled assistant as you are learning. It is not uncommon for an issue to involve more than one partial self: for example, there may be a second part that has a reaction to the first part, or doesn't want you to listen to that one. When that occurs, it's most useful to shift your attention and say "hello" to the new part, rather than trying to shut it out. Then proceed with the steps of the Inseeing Process, giving this new part an opportunity to say what it's concerned about. Once it has had a chance to be expressed, it will most likely relax so you can return to the first part and continue from where you left off.

With complex issues, there may be several parts showing up with their respective agendas. Although you may wish to give attention to all of them, in any given session there may not be enough time to do that. Instead, if a new part comes in and tries to talk over the part you're working with, you might imagine putting your arm around that part and telling it you will come back to it another time. Sometimes it takes several sessions to invite all the concerned parties, and hear what they want you to hear, in order to arrive in a place of resolution and fresh air.

Once you have achieved some familiarity with the steps of the Inseeing Process, you might enjoy practicing with a partner who is also learning this approach. The ability to tune in to what's going on internally is almost always enhanced by having another person listening deeply and reflecting your words back to you. At **divinelyhuman.com** you can find information about private sessions, upcoming classes, and a list of practitioners who incorporate this type of compassionate listening into their work with students and clients.

As you gain experience, you will naturally find that you begin being with yourself in a way that is also very inviting and healing. Although it may seem complicated at first, the steps of the Inseeing Process are actually very organic and intuitive. They will quickly become second nature. When you are with your feelings in this way, you are able to feel them without being overwhelmed by them, because you know they are not the whole of who you are.

For now let it suffice to say that compassionately being with your feelings gives them room to evolve into their natural optimal functioning, and will give you access to vast reservoirs of body wisdom. Being able to bring Presence to all that you are will also lay the foundation for your complete and irrevocable awakening into your whole divinely human self.

6

Presence

Our Story: Over time, we discovered a much greater ability to be fully in Presence with strong feelings, thoughts, and emotions, both our own and those of others. These strong feelings ran the full range of possibility, including sensual delights as well as more difficult feelings.

Holding self and others

"Holding" means staying fully present, warm, and responsive, while attending to inner parts of yourself or another person. When you are in a state of Presence rather than reactivity, all parties are held in love, and you can be available without being blown away.

Much as the practice of Inseeing cultivates your ability to bring warm, interested curiosity to inner parts of yourself that need some attention, by strengthening your ability to be in Presence you can bring that same kind of loving attention to other people, animals, or even plants, as well. This type of unconditional Presence is the most loving gift you can give to another being, because it makes room for them to be all that they are. In that space, they can come into their full, embodied aliveness.

Emotions are not a sign of weakness

We are often given the message that emotions, especially fear and sadness, are a sign of weakness. This comes from people who are weak themselves, who dislike feeling emotions in their body, perhaps because they were never given enough support to come into their own emotional maturity. They will tend to use the strategy of shaming to put others on the defensive. It is more true to say that emotional expression is a sign of strength and requires courage, especially in societies that do not have widespread acceptance of emotional expression.

Everyone needs to have their feelings seen and validated. If you feel an emotion but are told not to feel it, or that what you're feeling isn't warranted in the situation, you can feel split or crazy, and come to doubt your inner experience.

For example: you're feeling upset and someone tells you, "There's no reason to be upset. You're being irrational." This sort of response can cause you to doubt that what you're feeling is valid, setting up a cognitive dissonance between your gut feeling that something is wrong and what you're hearing with your ears. This can lead to confusion, inner conflict, or even shame that you might be feeling something inappropriate and unapproved by others.

We *need* to have our feelings acknowledged by others if we are to be healthy and fully functioning beings. When our feelings are met with mixed messages or negativity, we feel chaotic inside and distrust that our emotions can be good for us. We might conclude that emotions are just interior storms that make our lives more difficult.

The harm we do to self and others by avoiding feeling

Sadly, many, if not most, children are raised in situations where emotions are not well tolerated. They are threatened: "Stop crying this instant or I'll give you something to really cry about!" Or they are shamed: "Don't be a sissy." Or overpowered: "Shut up!" or "Children should be seen and not heard." Or they are told they ought to be feeling something different from what they are feeling: "Cheer up, it's not so bad. Look on the bright side!" Or in some homes, children are neglected or ignored, providing a perhaps subtler but no less damaging effect of inhibiting the full development of their ability to feel appropriate feelings and trust themselves in their thoughts and opinions.

Sound familiar? Most of us can easily remember similar situations from our childhood.

Boys are especially repressed

Tragically, this type of repression seems to be especially aimed at boys, while girls are given somewhat greater latitude for expressing their feelings. All too many boys grow up unable to discriminate various feelings because they have been punished or ridiculed whenever they expressed strong emotions. It's not that the emotions go away—they continue to show up in a sort of overwhelming rush, or uncomfortable mixture of feelings that are difficult to articulate. Then, in their desire to appear "together," young men try even harder to suppress their feelings, leading to a vicious cycle of avoidance and overwhelm. When one day they fall in love, suddenly their partners want and expect them to be able to communicate their feelings but they've never learned the language.

Girls suffer too, even though they have more leeway to be emotional in our society. They are often expected to be "irrational," as if they are helpless victims of emotions run amok. While they may be allowed to have emotional reactions, they are seldom taught how to bring discriminating awareness to their feelings in order to sort through or articulate them.

When kids' feelings are shamed or repressed, they can become emotionally handicapped well into adult life. What everyone needs in order to be emotionally healthy and coherent is clear reflection and validation by others. This is even more true for children, who are just beginning to learn how to experience the emotional richness of life. When a child is sad, what helps most is someone sitting with them and saying, in effect, "Yes, I see you are sad, and that sad feeling is appropriate right now." And the same applies to jubilation, fear, rage—the whole array of feeling-states. Although parents do need to set some boundaries on their children's expression of strong emotion, so that they are not acting out in hurtful ways, what children most need is to be seen and welcomed in the full range of their feelings.

The other side of suppression: acting out

While many people suppress their feelings, keeping them mostly bottled up inside, others swing to the opposite extreme, expressing and acting out their reactions at every turn. Some might even say they "inflict" their emotions—they express them dramatically without regard for the people around them.

It might seem at first glance that such expression is preferable to keeping emotions bottled up where they fester until something causes the top to blow off. However, acting out seldom provides anything more than a temporary release of pressure.

Recent research has shown that people can develop a kind of biochemical "addiction" to certain emotional states due to how their body adapts to their most predominant feelings. Someone who has been chronically depressed, or chronically angry, develops more biochemical receptors for those particular emotions than other types. The "familiar" states are then more easily triggered than other states that have less biochemical signals available, and this accounts for why some people appear to be very stuck in repetitively acting out their particular dramas.

Neither suppression nor expression has the power to bring healing energy to the patterns that are driving the emotional reactions. Healing requires awareness.

Emotions and intuitions are your aliveness

Why would you want to feel emotions anyway? Emotions and their counterpart body sensations give color, depth, and fullness to your experience of life, bringing it into a vivid, 3-D richness that would be much shallower if you did not feel them. We all feel emotions even if we don't know a lot about them. They bring us essential information about our lives and what we need in order to live consciously and be fulfilled. If your emotions are absent, as they can be with some kinds of depression or illness, you will feel very flat, as if something vital is missing from your life.

On the other hand, when you feel moved by beauty, touched by a poignant movie, heartbroken when you lose a loved one, swept away in the early throes of romance, or thrilled on a roller coaster, you feel especially alive. It is your ability to feel deeply that brings meaning into your life.

There are no right or wrong or good or bad feelings

Because some emotions, such as happiness or love, are more pleasurable in the body than others, we have formed the tendency to label—and oversimplify—emotions as being either "good" or "bad." And we then tend to go for one of two options. One option is to try to increase what we perceive as "good" feelings and get rid of the so-called "bad" ones. There are many self-help gurus who promise you the keys to unending happiness—but the failure rate of these programs is high.

The other option is to try to get some distance from emotions, period. Some meditation or other spiritual practices teach people to pull back from emotions and simply witness them as if looking down from a mountain peak. The promise of these programs is equanimity and inner peace. Although they can bring some relief from the distress of chronic unhappiness, the relief often comes at a price of reduced aliveness. We have the capacity to experience the full range of what is possible for us as humans. Why cut that off?

The shadow side of positive thinking

The tendency to prefer "good" over "bad" shows up in our thinking as well. Since thoughts and emotions can be highly correlated, many self-help programs encourage you to think only positive thoughts in order to create the life you want. While there is real merit in becoming able to notice your thoughts—and therefore your conditioned ways of thinking—a potential shadow side of such programs is that you become afraid of your so-called "negative thinking," as if it will bring about a horrible outcome in your life. Or, should you experience a painful situation or disease, you might unduly blame yourself for creating your problem through "negative" thoughts.

We need to look below the surface level of teachings that tell us to change our thoughts in order to change how we feel and how our life will turn out. We are more complex than most self-help manuals would really acknowledge—just ask any therapist. And we actually have very little control over what pops up in our minds, or what emotions arise. They simply appear! And although we can draw some correlations between persistent attitudes we hold about the world and our current experience, for most people it is not possible to "decide" to think only positive thoughts and then succeed at it.

But you know what? In my experience, the vast majority of our thoughts do NOT create anything other than themselves in the moment. It is the deeper patterns of our conditioning that tend to create repetitious situations in our lives, where we feel stuck and disempowered.

Willingness to FEEL without FIXING

When someone is willing to *feel* without trying to *fix*, a very magical alchemy is unleashed. Such non-intrusive contact is one of the most powerful healing forces available to you. It not only gives you the opportunity to notice what you are feeling, but this positive attention also helps you focus long enough to get to the deeper layers and meaning of your experience, where buried feelings can be brought into the light. Again, once those deeper layers are seen and felt, the natural healing mechanism of your conscious inner body kicks in and moves the whole situation toward wholeness.

This happens without any need to *try to make* anything change. In fact, it is the very pressure to change that so often locks things in place. Whatever is arising in your internal experience has an important message for you, and until you receive that message in your conscious awareness, it will persist in trying to get through, resisting all efforts to change it or make it go away. This is why so many people fail to achieve lasting success with affirmations that attempt to override negative thoughts by pasting positive thoughts over them. Or they fail to be able to maintain a peaceful equanimity, for much the same reason. What is arising in your mind and emotional body is relevant even when unpleasant, and it needs to be listened to from a state of Presence in order to create an environment where healing can occur. Then new possibilities open up spontaneously, without effort.

Freedom

Real freedom is the freedom to spontaneously experience the full range of life, including all feelings, all thoughts, all states of being, sickness and health, and failure and success. It is in the play of opposites that we get to understand and value our experience. For instance, love is all the more sweet after we have experienced loss. And health is all the more appreciated after there has been illness. And for that matter, think of flavors: if sweet was the only flavor we encountered, we'd lose the ability to notice it. Sweetness is all the more special when it comes as a contrast to salty, bitter, sour, or savory. Therefore, it is to our ultimate benefit not to be cutting any of it off, since we never know what the next moment will bring.

Sensual delights

If your life has been overly-skewed to the side of pain, disappointment, and suffering, you will naturally seek RELIEF—some way to make the pain go away and stay gone. But dissociation from painful feelings means dissociation from pleasure as well, and that is a price you may not want to pay. The alternative is to do your interior work. As you heal and release the backlog of old pain from the past you will simultaneously open the door to more sensual pleasure in the here and now.

You can begin today. Make a practice of noticing the little things that make your body smile and say "Yes!"—and then experiment with doing them more often. It may be taking a walk on a mild day, listening to a favorite CD through headphones, eating a bowl of ice cream, or enjoying leisurely lovemaking. For those of you who've been told that spiritual progress requires self-discipline and a denial of the desires of the flesh, this recommendation may come as a surprise, but self-denial is of limited benefit. For awakening in an *embodied* fashion, you need to reconnect the impaired lines of communication between your head and your body. You will need to be able to hear your body's healthy signals, learn from them, and respond appropriately. We're not advocating becoming blind hedonists. What we have discovered, however, is that getting into the sensual delights of life will give you a more balanced perspective, open you to more pleasure, happiness, and joy, and help restore hope that life is more than endless suffering, sorrow, or defeat.

Emotional flow

When you are emotionally and mentally healthy, thoughts and feelings come and go easily. Think of children and how they are crying one minute in great distress and then laughing easily with delight in the next minute. This is the potential of greenlighting ALL of your feelings: they get freed up to flow more easily from one to the next and to the next. And you discover that it wasn't so much that you needed to feel good all the time, as that you had become stuck in uncomfortable states, such as inner confusion, chaos, self-doubt, or overwhelm.

Real change *is* possible—and has happened in many people just like you—but it takes time and persistence and compassion for yourself in the process. It begins exactly where you are now in this moment, with the open encountering of whatever is showing up in a way that greenlights it both to *be as it is*, as well as to change and evolve. Remember, *what is seen and felt moves*. When you permit yourself to consciously *experience* the felt sense of whatever is up for you—not just thinking about and telling the story over and over—you create the optimum environment for backed up energy to dissipate, clarity to return, and new, creative responses to become available.

Three states: identifying (merging), exiling, and Presence

The best way to cope with being an emotional being is to develop a strong ability to be in Presence with your feelings, thoughts, and reactions. What usually happens instead is automatically identifying with particular emotions while automatically distancing from other emotions.

When you're identified (merged) with an emotion, you'll tend to state the feeling strongly: "I'm so pissed right now!" or "I'm scared!" or "I'm so sad I feel like I could lie down and die."

On the other hand, if you're dissociated from (exiling) an emotion you might say, "I'm NOT angry!" through your clenched teeth. Or you might permit yourself to feel an acceptable feeling but not a stronger underlying feeling.

Example: someone who thinks it's not permissible to feel or express anger might report feeling very sad or even depressed, when underneath that they are actually quite angry but unable to allow themselves to acknowledge that feeling. They are denying the anger, and pretending it isn't there.

When you are either merged with a part, or exiling some aspect of your makeup, you have little access to help that part of you grow, become integrated, or transform.

The third option, the one that has the greatest power to free up bound energy and bring integration, is to *be in Presence with* the broken zones and partial selves, seeing and feeling them without either assuming that they are all of who you are, or being in denial that you are having the feeling in the first place. Presence provides warm, interested attention, and is spacious enough to allow *all* of you to be here, without needing to force any aspect of yourself to change or go away.

Presence says, "I see you there. Welcome. I care and I am listening. You are a part of me, yet not all of what I am." Presence provides just enough distance for you to fully experience whatever's arising in you without being overwhelmed or lost in it.

Presence is being present, and something more. . .

When you begin learning how to observe your reactions and conditioned behaviors, you realize that there is a mysterious aspect of yourself that can watch in a dispassionate, though loving, manner. This *something* doesn't take sides but instead has almost infinite capacity to simply register all the different aspects of what is going on in your life, both inner and outer, and be with them without pulling away, shutting down, or condemning.

Presence, as I'm defining the term, is that which gives you the ability to hold yourself with compassion. It is a natural state that is inherent in everyone, but it is often hidden from awareness when you are more attuned to the objects and events around you than to the subtle essence that is doing the observing. When you begin to notice and employ Presence in your life, its powerful light becomes more and more available.

What Presence actually is cannot really be known by the mind, but you can sense Presence in your body as spaciousness, flow, or aliveness. And it can be experienced as that which holds self and others, even in our/their most difficult places. Presence is infinite, unlimited, and spiritual, which is why I use a capital "P" when writing it.

Even more than a state of awareness, Presence is infinite Consciousness itself as it interacts with our human bodies. You can learn to use Presence no matter what your current stage of unfoldment, but it will be transient, like all states, until, with embodied awakening, the light of Presence is switched on in you, never to be turned off again.

Presence is associative, not dissociative

Presence is up close and personal, even though we are talking about an utterly intangible Mystery. It is related to, but different from, the transcendent, dissociated Witnessing that is described in much of spiritual literature. Presence does not watch from a distance and thereby remove the highs and lows from one's experience; it is right here in the midst of it. "Presence" as I'm using the term is *embodied* Awareness. It is here-now, an aliveness that is intimately associated with all of the elements of our human experience. As the ultimate Observer of all experience, it is the aspect of our being that is not limited to our personal sphere but is actually unbounded and infinite, unable to be pinned down or described in any finite sort of way. And as such, it is this Presence that is our very connection with what we call *divine*—that ineffable, infinite, all-pervasive Mystery of existence.

The cabinet minister analogy

I like to think of the host of inner voices and partial selves that surface into my awareness as allies. In the past, they were often petty tyrants that caused a lot of turmoil, chaos, agitation, and reactivity in my life. But when I awoke to my true and total Self, bit by bit something much greater began to occupy the central position of who I am, as if it were the President of the country of me. Instead of exiling all those formerly-petty tyrants, this President gave them seats in the cabinet—they became advisors. They give all sorts of advice that the President listens to respectfully. When all sides have weighed in, the President is free to take whatever action is appropriate in the moment. In this manner, all of the aspects of the total Self work together in a seamless unity that includes access to useful information from the past, assessment of the current situation, and freedom to take action informed, but not limited, by what was experienced in the past.

A messy process

Awakening is messy and unpredictable. In some ways, it's like the pins and needles you get when a part of your body had "gone to sleep" and now circulation is returning: it can be a prickly process! In most cases, we've suppressed far more than our emotions—we've suppressed the most tender, true parts of ourselves as well. The process of inviting our innermost essence forward must necessarily involve inviting ALL of ourselves forward—the good, the bad, the ugly. The beautiful! *All* of what we are needs to feel welcome here in order to create the internal space for our divine Conscious nature to embody. The more open you are to your innermost thoughts, feelings, and attitudes, the more you will also be open to the tender authentic essence of yourself that is coming alive, as well as to the vastness of your divine nature.

It's bound to be a messy process. It's not possible to do it neatly. The Inseeing Process, and the power of Presence which is behind it, are useful tools to help you get a line on the parts of you that are coming up into the light of your awareness. Inseeing is inherently greenlighting of whatever comes—welcoming it with interested curiosity.

But you will no doubt discover that you simply can't, or don't want to, welcome everything (including other people's stuff) *all* the time. There will be times when you're triggered and totally immersed in whatever emotion is happening, and unwilling or unable to do anything more than just *be that*. That's all right! It's a natural part of this remarkable whole-being transformative process you're engaging in. There will be times when Presence eludes you, and that's okay.

It's more than okay, even. By offering these techniques, I do not mean to suggest that you should be doing them all the time, or that you should be striving to do the "right" thing and be a good student of divinely human awakening. If you try to figure it out and always do it right, that very action will put a damper on the wild current that is switching on in you, and that would not be helpful. It is important to remember not to hold Presence as some ideal that you then make a fetish out of, or judge yourself for failing to accomplish when you are not experiencing it. Presence is fundamental to your nature, but your ability to be aware of it will come and go until that recognition becomes fully established and unshakable. Once this is the case, there will be no going back.

The bottom line is that you feel what you feel, and there is no need to try to fight your divinely *human* nature. Instead, when you greenlight and hold yourself in your experience—including when you are *not* in Presence—real transformation and healing take place. Huge amounts of backed-up energy from years of suppressing emotions begins to get released through the process of consciously allowing yourself to feel and speak what was left incomplete in the past. And as this energy is released, healing begins. Instead of being like a full balloon, ready to pop whenever pricked, you become more liked Play Dough—soft and stretchy, able to adapt to arising situations without losing your integrity of being.

Presence language

You invite Presence whenever you attend to what is going on in your inner life, and whenever you invite your thoughts and feelings as if they are important members of your cabinet. When you send an inner acknowledgment to a feeling, letting it know that you are aware of it, it is Presence that is sending that acknowledgment. Similarly, when you let it know that you have heard its message, it is Presence that is doing the hearing. Even when you are fully immersed in strong feeling states, Presence is there registering all that is happening, and in time its light will help to bring about a healing of whatever trauma patterns were formed in the past. When you practice Inseeing, you will discover a means of articulating your experience that honors both the human and the divine aspects of what you are. No longer will you identify solely with the conditioned, reactive aspect. By bringing patient, curious Presence to whatever is arising, you can't help but realize that the totality of What You Are is greater than any of your parts. You begin not only to taste your divinely human nature, but to live it.

Try this: Presence language

When practicing the steps of the Inseeing Process, begin using Presence language to help you remember that you are bigger than the issue you are investigating. For instance:

- I'm sensing
- I'm noticing
- I'm aware of
- I'm realizing
- I'm recognizing
- I'm seeing/hearing
- I'm saying hello to it
- I'm sensing how it feels
- I'm letting it know I heard it
- I'm thanking what's come

And don't forget those three magic words you learned in Chapter 4 that really make a difference in how you relate to what's arising. They are "something in me." When you identify an issue as "something in me," you acknowledge it as a part of you, yet also acknowledge that it might not have the complete picture of your life. There is a bigger aspect of your whole-being self that is able to be aware of the issue, and listen to it with interested curiosity. Try it out when you practice Inseeing and see the difference it can make when you say, "I'm sensing something in me that..." It's a distinction that will really help bring Presence alive for you.

One step at a time

Learning to be in Presence with your feelings, thoughts, reactions, remembrances of past traumas, and anxieties for the future takes patience and a willingness to feel uncomfortable at times. Presence grows with practice. Although it is already a part of who you are, it cannot become a living force in your life until you begin tuning into it and welcoming it. Whenever you remember that you are more than your conditioned self, you strengthen Presence and its power in your life.

In this chapter we explored Presence as an active force for your own awakening process and for supporting others as well. People *need* this type of deep holding to be able to cope well with the strong feeling-states that accompany being divinely human. Contrary to popular spiritual lore, embodied awakening often brings greater intensity of feeling and more emotion, not less. In the absence of holding from others, we can feel lost, alone, separate, alienated, and often hopeless. This step is about learning to really help ourselves and one another be here.

At first, you will probably want and need skillful helpers to model this for you. As you are held and greenlighted by others from Presence, you will gradually become more able to greenlight your own thoughts and feelings by yourself. And once you begin giving yourself this deep listening, you will naturally, in turn, begin doing it for others as well. When you offer the gift of your Presence, honesty, and authenticity to others, everyone is enriched in the process. This is a very real, tangible way to help bring about an end to violence while bringing more love into the world, person by person, body by body, heart by heart. We will explore the self/other dynamic more fully in the chapter on Mutuality. Meanwhile, our next chapter will discuss some ways you can get conscious support for your own awakening process.

7

SUPPORT

Our Story: We sought out and joined together with like-minded people who were also committed to the love, investigation, and expression of true and total Being. Whenever possible, we worked closely with divinely human teachers and other helpers, to benefit from their Presence, experience, and transmission.

The importance of good company

The project of becoming divinely human is one that is quite challenging and fraught with unknowns and pitfalls along the way. And while books can be very helpful in describing the territory that will be traveled, there is no substitute for a skilled, wise guide who has traveled ahead and is now willing to help you make the journey. In this chapter, we will discuss some of the benefits of working with teachers, mentors, and other types of support. We will also cover some of the hazards that can be encountered in the teacher-student relationship, and how they can be avoided—or at least managed for the most optimal results.

You can't do it alone—not fully anyway

On your own, you can only go so far in your inner journeys. This may be quite far—indeed, some people have profound, fundamental awakenings without the benefit of a teacher or community. Still, the full flowering of such an awakening comes in the company of other awakened and awakening people. There is a special value in being able to express your discoveries, and hear others' revelations. When you are practicing independently, there is no one to mirror your blind spots back to you, or to show you a vision of something possible that you had not considered before. You will inevitably be limited in some ways if you don't open yourself to awakened companionship.

Just having information about awakening is not sufficient for most people. You might have various kinds of openings, mystical experiences, or deep recognitions that feel life-changing in the moment, but what typically occurs is that these experiences are short-lived and fade into the background leaving confusion or discouragement in their wake. Once you enter the dark night (whether deconstructing happens in a dramatic, or subtle, manner), you will be best served by a personal approach— personal contact with a teacher who can see you and respond to your unique attributes and unique process of embodied awakening. Blanket recommendations and formulaic processes have their place, but once you have hit the wall and are being undone by life, personal attention becomes especially important.

Another very important reason to build a support system into your life is that there will come times during your awakening process when you may well be "reduced" to your most broken places, even to the extent of feeling you are on the brink of primal insanity. This can be a scary time, when you'll be thankful to have already established some trustable relationships, ones that can be stronger than the compelling illogic of your broken zones.

The unhealthy aspects of co-dependency have been well publicized, leading some people to avoid turning to others for support. Instead, they swing far in the other direction and isolate themselves. But there is a middle ground of healthy *interdependence,* where all parties remain responsible for their own lives, yet able to engage with one another for support and growth. Divinely human interdependence leaves plenty of room for individual expression and autonomy, yet includes opportunities for mutual interaction where the divine essence of each person is seen, acknowledged, and valued.

Now, how do you find a teacher or other helper who understands *embodied* awakening? I recommend working only with those who a) have had an embodied awakening themselves, b) really understand the power of greenlighting, and c) can help you learn effective ways to work with your inner process.

A teacher or counselor with a divinely human orientation will primarily greenlight and support, rather than criticize, offer so-called "constructive" feedback, or point out your ego or other so-called "negative" aspects of your character. They will offer non-judging reflection to help you become more self-aware. And they will come from a fundamental trust that your life is unfolding in an organic and intelligent way, guided by Being. They realize their job is primarily to keep you company along the way, rather than tell you what you should think or do.

The Waking Down Community

The place where I have found a lot of folks who meet these criteria is my "home base" community of Waking Down in Mutuality. There is an association of awakened-and-embodied teachers (the Waking Down Teachers Association) and a school for training prospective mentors and teachers (the Institute of Awakened Mutuality), and there are local community groups in a number of places in North America and overseas. This interlinked community has developed a model of supportive relationships that has proven very effective at fostering embodied awakenings, a model that can help you awaken, too.

We've found that personal coaching has been a key ingredient in successful embodied awakenings, so we typically offer one-on-one and small-group personalized attention from people who are able to meet you exactly where you are in your process, and help guide you toward your most auspicious unfolding. The limitation of most "guru-on-the-stage" situations, where the same advice is being given out to everyone in the room, is that what is right for you at one time may be quite ineffective at other stages of your awakening process. The only way for a teacher to help you determine what's right for you *now* is by knowing and interacting with you individually.

The heart of my personal teaching work is the radical embrace of everything, and this is also the foundation of Waking Down in Mutuality. Beyond that, I, like other teachers of this approach, have developed my own way of teaching and working with students that in some ways diverges from what we might call the "core dharma"—so don't be surprised if other teachers have different ways of talking about Waking Down. We are learning more about conscious embodiment all the time, and one of the exciting things about Waking Down is the opportunity to share our discoveries with one another and thus grow as a body of practice. We are becoming more like a university with a collection of complementary teachings, than a single teaching put forth by any one teacher. That said, this chapter will introduce you to the practices that we've found most highly effective in helping Waking Down students land in permanent, integrated embodied awakenings.

Existential equality with functional hierarchy

Senior Waking Down teacher Krishna Gauci coined this phrase to convey the way we recognize both equality and hierarchy. As a community founded upon principles of mutuality, it stands to reason that we would hold a high regard for everyone's value as existential equals. Because we are all fundamentally both divine and human, it's true that we are all of equal value as people. In one way of looking at it, no one's experience is "more true" or "more right" than anyone else's.

On the other hand, we acknowledge a real difference in the skills we have in the practice of Waking Down in Mutuality, and in the perspectives we are able to hold. For instance, once someone has had a divinely human, "second birth" realization, their capacity for being able to hold themselves and others increases. And once someone trains to become a mentor, they have developed another degree of that capacity. Likewise for the teachers as they progress from interning teachers to full teachers to senior teachers. They deepen not only in capacity but also in skill, experience, and hard-won wisdom. Therefore we do acknowledge a functional hierarchy—in other words, real differences in skills and experience.

Introducing the support team: teachers, mentors, peers, therapists

The embodied awakening process brings buried feelings or deep-seated issues to the surface to help liberate the energy bound up in them, and thus facilitate whole-being awakening and integration. Therefore, to make your passage as easeful as possible, it's a good idea to have a support team consisting of a teacher, a mentor, a body-centered therapist who is oriented toward green-lighting, and peers who are at more or less similar stages of the awakening process as you.

Teachers of Waking Down are people who have been awake to their divinely human condition long enough to have completed significant integration and also to have gone through a training program that was especially focused on developing skills of holding, transmission, mutuality, and discriminating the stages of the embodied awakening process. They are strongly motivated to assist others in coming to the same realizations that have blessed and transformed their own lives.

Mentors have experienced the "second birth" shift and find themselves moved to volunteer their support to others in their awakening process. Many (though not all) of them aspire to become teachers and are mentoring as a part of their own training and integration. We generally think of mentors as "older sisters and brothers on the path"—folks who've walked the territory and are available for mutual conversation and support. They offer their services at no charge other than a requested modest donation to a scholarship fund.

Peers are those who are more or less at a similar place in their spiritual unfoldment as you are, with whom you can share your experiences along the way as friends on the path. An especially potent way to benefit from peer relationships is by being Inseeing partners for one another as described in Chapter 5.

Another valuable way to interact with peers is by participating in a regular **mutuality group**. This could be a teacher-led group (often called a *sitting*), or a group that meets without a teacher. Both types provide rich opportunities for practice in speaking one's truth and holding others who are doing the same. Mutuality groups can meet in person or via conference calls when the participants are not local to one another. There will be more information about mutuality groups in Chapter 8.

Therapists are especially helpful when you are encountering your more entrenched patterns or deep-seated issues. But all therapy is not the same, and it would be counterproductive to be working with a therapist who holds a "fix it" orientation that would work against the divinely human approach of greenlighting and radical acceptance.

Fortunately, some of the Waking Down teachers and mentors are also licensed therapists. In general, we've found that body-centered therapies provide the best support for embodied awakening, including but not limited to the modalities of Inseeing, Inner-Relationship Focusing, Hakomi, and Core Energetics. And for healing deep traumas, EMDR and Somatic Experiencing are especially useful. Working in any of these areas can provide a deep enrichment and enlivenment of your process.

If you find yourself at this point feeling a bit overwhelmed at the prospect of so much interpersonal support, remember that these are simply recommendations and that you remain the authority for your life and process. At every point, you determine the level of support that feels best to you.

Finding and working with a teacher

You are encouraged, if you find yourself drawn to this approach, to find *your* personal teacher. As there are quite a number to choose from, there's a good chance that you will find someone whose style, teaching, and personality appeal to you. Some are better at holding people in their brokenness, others at helping to clarify Consciousness. Still others might be able to relate to a particular spiritual framework that you know well, like having a background in Advaita Vedanta, Christianity, or 12-step programs.

It is important to find someone you resonate with. What does that mean? It means that when you are working with this person, most of the time you feel like they get who you are, that they are championing your fullest unfoldment, that you can understand what they are trying to communicate, and that you feel a reasonable degree of safety with them. Sometimes resonance feels a bit like falling in love, like something in your being just recognizes this person as "the one" who will serve you well.

While it is most useful to find and work with one primary teacher who can really get to know you and your process, the other side of the equation is that each teacher is unique and has a different background and skill set. It's not unusual for Waking Down aspirants to spend time with different teachers at different stages of their process.

Since sessions conducted by telephone are also quite effective, you don't have to be limited due to geographic considerations. You might meet a teacher at a workshop or a retreat, or you can visit **wakingdown.org/teachers** and read the teachers' personal pages to get a sense of who might be a fit for you. If you live near a teacher, he or she may be conducting local sittings or other classes you can attend as a way to get to know them.

Some people find that talking with their teacher every week is optimal. Others find that bi-weekly or even monthly is sufficient. Teachers generally request a flat fee for their time, so you'll want to make an arrangement that works for you financially.

Once you are working with a teacher, you are invited to also take advantage of the support of a volunteer mentor. Information about currently available mentors can be found at **wakingdown.org/mentors.**

Confidentiality

Information that is shared with Waking Down teachers and mentors or within group settings is considered confidential, and participants are all requested to not repeat personal details outside of that setting. There is an exception made within the teacher/ mentor community wherein a teacher or mentor may share with other teachers something about a student's process (without revealing unnecessary personal details) in order to serve them in the most useful manner. Feel free to discuss the parameters of confidentiality with anyone you are working with and be sure that you are comfortable and feel safe.

Your discoveries matter

In interactions with your teacher or others in the community, your truth is important and welcome. When you are undertaking something as profound and transformative as awakening your divinely human nature, the discoveries you are making on your own are equally important to whatever wisdom your teacher might share with you. What you discover for yourself becomes real for you, whereas what you hear from others is only conceptual unless and until it clicks into place for you personally.

It is also useful (and not considered disrespectful in our work) to speak any questions, doubts, fears, or resistance when that's up for you. This may include skepticism that this approach will really work, or perhaps distrust of the skill, motivations, or even ethics of a teacher. Do bring it up. Speak it! Speaking these things will take you most directly to your "edges"—those aspects of who you are that are wanting more light—and help you sort out what's true now from what is left over from times you've been hurt in the past, or witnessed others being hurt.

You may well have good reason to distrust. It is a tragic fact that a number of spiritual leaders have had lapses of judgment or poor ethical boundaries, and have brought disillusionment—even devastation—to those who trusted them as guides. Or perhaps you've had experience with another person who was untrustworthy, such as an abusive or erratic parent, teacher, or other authority figure. Whether you have been personally affected or only heard about these abuses of power second-hand, you may understandably be reluctant to open yourself to anyone in a similar role. This is as it should be! If you are not feeling trust, that is not a failing or weakness on your part, but a healthy instinct to avoid further injury. Since your doubts may, however, keep you from fully receiving the benefits of transmission from awakened helpers, it will be useful, when you are ready and feel *safe enough*, to begin speaking them in an appropriate way, so they can be resolved and trust can grow.

Teachers are not all-knowing

Teachers are not all-knowing or always right. Teachers are divinely human beings who remain imperfect and fallible, and at times you might find yourself really wondering if there's anything "divine" about them at all. They will get triggered and go through hard times. They might fail to really get you sometimes. They might do something that hurts your feelings. It's not that embodied teachers are more messed up than other types of spiritual teachers or leaders; rather, it's simply that they've made a choice not to hide their humanness from the people they serve.

At first, this might seem incongruous. If you see a teacher in pain, or reacting to something and showing anything but equanimity, you might question what qualifies that person to be a teacher for you. You might even question whether they have actually awakened, especially if you hold to the myth that awakening brings a constant state of inner peace and grace. But we're talking about **embodied** awakenings here, and that means the awakening is inclusive of all of our humanity, including the messy parts we sometimes wish we did not have. By allowing students to see that they, too, are vulnerable and can experience doubts, fears, anger, grief—the entire range of feelings—teachers are demonstrating that this awakening is very down to earth, very real, and very attainable by ordinary folk leading ordinary lives. Like you and me.

The community of Waking Down in Mutuality has seen its share of messy interactions. We freely admit that we are not perfectly able to live up to our own ideals all of the time. What is rather unique here, however, is that the teachers are willing to let you see them as they are, and are willing to take feedback about their behavior, especially if you feel you have been injured by one of them. Then they will do their best to be accountable and make amends.

Teachers are not therapists (with some exceptions)

Waking Down teachers are not therapists. Not only are they not trained in the diagnosis and treatment of specific psychological disorders, they are not bound to keep their personal feelings private, as are therapists. When you work with a licensed therapist, the focus is on you and the therapist typically will not bring their personal experience into the relationship. However, the goals of working with a Waking Down teacher are quite different—they're not about fixing what ails you, but about helping you come fully alive and awake in all your divinely human glory, exactly as you are. We have found that it is more useful for your teacher to meet you as a fellow traveler on this journey, with a degree of give and take in the interaction that can help you template off of the real, lived, awakened condition of the teacher.

Note: *since most of the teachers in the Waking Down community are NOT licensed therapists (although some are), they do not have the training to address serious psychological situations. Spiritual teaching is not therapy, even though it may involve helping you learn many things about how you function as a human being. If the going gets rough in your awakening process (as often happens at some point), do seek out appropriately skilled professional assistance.*

You remain the authority for your own life— like it or not

Although we encourage aspirants to work with a number of helpers along the way, we also remind them that they are the authority in their own life. Awakening into your divinely human life involves stepping into a deeper recognition of your own autonomy, even while forming lines of connection and interdependence. In the final analysis, no one but you can know what is going on in you, or what you truly need.

At times you may feel insecure, self-doubting, and vulnerable in this bewildering world. Your teachers and mentors are here to support you, but not to tell you what decisions to make for your life. That is always in your hands. What we will do is help you learn how to sort out the threads and various elements of your life in order to be able to make good choices. And we will help you tailor a program to support your most auspicious progress through the inevitably difficult passages you will encounter. But we will not tell you what to do—even if you ask us to!

Due diligence

You are advised to do some "due diligence" with all the members of your support team—and with the embodiment approach itself. It's possible that the divinely human path might not be right for you at this time, but might be at another time, in a different phase of your unfoldment. Due diligence also means finding out if this is a "safe enough" place for you to grow and prosper. You'll want to check things out before getting too involved. Wait a while to see how things operate, and what level of commitment the practitioners have to each other's growth in a mutually safe environment. For example, how well do they work through difficult issues between people?

You will also want to know what values are held by the community, and their agreements about ethical conduct between teachers and students. No one can be *perfectly* safe, but what's most important is that they show a level of consideration for you that leaves you feeling safe enough to be willing to take some risks, because the rewards from such risk-taking can be profoundly valuable to you over time.

Feel free to shop around until you find the teacher or other helper whose approach works for you. Different teachers have different styles, and if you don't like what's happening with one teacher, you are welcome—and advised—to find another.

Issues of devotion and attraction

Feelings of devotion and attraction can easily arise when you are working with teachers or mentors in this work. When you find that special connection with someone who is the embodiment of the divine in human form, who really sees and gets the divinely human being that *you* are, it can feel rather like falling in love. It is natural for hearts to be touched and feelings of attraction to go along with that, especially since this is an embodiment process, wherein students are encouraged to invite their feelings to be present and acknowledged, and also are reconnecting their body-awareness with their mental awareness. Given all that, and that awakening itself often starts one's juices flowing, it is not unexpected for people to find themselves feeling awash in love, gratitude, or devotion for those who are supporting them deeply. These powerful feelings can provide further energy for the awakening process as long as they are held with care, within appropriate boundaries.

Re-parenting

Waking Down teachers work with you in a re-parenting fashion to help supply elements that might have been missing in your early development. These elements, on the mothering side, may include seeing you as you really are, unconditional positive regard, and radical acceptance of all of you, including the good, the bad, and the ugly. On the fathering side, there may be leadership, boundary-setting, and wise guidance. This kind of conscious mothering and fathering will turn up in your work with any teacher to greater or lesser degrees, regardless of whether they are a man or a woman.

Working together in this fashion will inevitably trigger areas of pain from your childhood at some point. There's a natural tendency to project a sort of two-dimensional "ideal parent" image upon a teacher, which will last only as long as the teacher doesn't touch any of your hot buttons. One day you'll be delighting in the "good mothering" energy you are receiving, then another day you may find yourself suddenly experiencing your teacher as "bad mother" or "bad father" due to some inadvertent comment or perceived slight, and be tempted to break off with them at that point. But it is exactly at these moments when breakthroughs and profound openings can occur.

Triggering of regression into child states is actually useful for healing, because it is precisely when you are fully immersed in the "young" feeling state that *experiencing a different result* can make the biggest impact on your whole-being understanding. It can release the old energy and free it for something new to become true for you. This is not to say that your teachers intentionally take you into areas of pain and wounding, but that such types of triggering are an entirely normal, and potentially very potent, part of the process of engaging with teachers.

We can only go so far with our inner work if we are doing it in isolation from others. At some point, we are going to find ourselves in a situation with others where our past wounding comes flaring into life, bringing all of its confusion and distress with it. Rather than avoid such situations, it is highly beneficial to regard these moments as points of power. Staying in communication at such times is a key element, one that can make all the difference between simply getting re-triggered and in having a healing experience. Remember that the people on your support team are there to help you achieve some breathing room in the midst of your conditioned responses to life, in order to create space for *all* of who you are to come alive, even the most shy, tender parts. When your "surrogate parent" teacher stays in communication with you, and is able and willing to hear your distress without breaking off contact, you are receiving a different result than what happened in the past. Your whole wiring begins to get reconfigured.

However, when situations like this flare up, it may be very difficult to sort things through with the person with whom you are experiencing the triggering. That's why it's useful to have more than one person on your support team. When things get sticky with one person, you can turn to another person on your team for help in gaining perspective on the feelings that are arising. This is not a substitute for bringing your feedback directly to the teacher who has triggered you. You will be encouraged to do that, but in your own time and readiness to do so.

Living fire

Awakening is potent stuff. It's dynamite. It's volcanic. It's a tectonic force at work to rewire your whole being to be able to run more voltage than ever before, due to your spiritual energy body coming fully on line. It's dancing with fire while trying not to get burned. It's not child's play, nor is it for the faint-hearted. In the final analysis, it is the ultimate hero's journey, and may well require you to tap inner resources you never knew you had. This is your "surgeon general's warning" that embarking on a path of awakening is risky business and will bring about profound changes in your life, some of which will have utterly unpredictable outcomes and consequences.

If you have read this far you are very likely finding yourself already self-enrolled and sliding down the slippery slope of your own manifest destiny as a divinely human being. Bravo! We are glad to have your company in this amazing adventure.

Your teachers have the challenge of creating a safe-enough space—a cradle for your awakening—while also greenlighting the living fire of your divinity taking human form, whatever that may bring forth in the process. It is vitally important that participants in this work have plenty of room to ignite, to explode, to get into the room, whatever it takes. Too many "rules" or codes of behavior are counterproductive to that process. This applies to teachers as well, as too many rules or restrictions on *their* behavior would deprive you of seeing them in their own raw brilliance (and messiness). There isn't a "right" way to awaken here, and as you will be discovering, becoming divinely human means that you become more *you*, not necessarily more "nice," or more of what anyone else (or *you*) would like you to be. That's not the point. The point is for you to *get here*, take a stand for yourself, and be willing to make an impact while you are here, however that looks—and whether or not those around you are appreciating it in the moment.

This does NOT mean that our goal is for everyone to become self-absorbed assholes. Getting here is Step 1, and becoming aware of how we impact others is Step 2. But Step 1 does seem to require more self-absorption and self-assertion than many spiritual paths would seem to condone. But that's how it is in this work. You need to cut yourself loose to discover who you are.

Potential teacher-student problems

So this is what counterbalances the picture of your awakened helpers as "good parents." Yes, they will be that for you to some degree. But never forget that they, too, are aflame with the living fire of awakened spirit. And they are walking the fine line that includes an internal demand for self-expression on the one hand, and an acute sensitivity to the Other that they have been cultivating in order to serve people in the awakening process.

Spiritual teachers, as is true for other people in positions of authority and trust, can be tempted to abuse that trust, especially in the areas of sexuality, money, and power. Collectively, we (teachers and mentors) have learned through hard-won experience that certain restraints on self-expression are essential to creating a *sufficient* climate of safety for people to awaken. So it is wise for anyone who is considering working with a spiritual teacher to be aware of these potential problem areas. When both teachers and students are working together to hold agreed-upon boundaries, the likelihood of abuse goes down dramatically.

The WDTA

This is one of the reasons the Waking Down teachers have joined together to create the Waking Down Teachers Association. We realize that, acting alone, spiritual teachers may feel they have no one to answer to except themselves. But there have been too many painful lapses of integrity on the part of spiritual teachers, across many traditions and paths, in recent years to think that anyone is completely impervious to temptation. Anyone can fall into a blind spot without warning, because a blind spot is just that—a pattern of behavior that is invisible to us until someone can help us see it through conscious reflection. Most such blind spots and broken zones are fairly benign, but when they involve intimate contact with vulnerable students, the results can be traumatic not only for the student, but also for the teacher, the people around them, and the entire community.

As an association of awakened spiritual teachers, the members of the WDTA voluntarily agree to comply with an ethics policy that outlines our boundaries around sexual and romantic relationships, money, and power. Equally, or even more importantly, we have all agreed to stay in mutuality with one another. This means that all teachers meet together in groups of 4 to 6 on a regular basis, and share what is happening in our personal lives and in our teaching work. In this fashion, we build networks of relationships that provide a rich field of support for our own ongoing development as teachers and as divinely human beings.

And we also have a system in place that can help spot potential problem areas and provide assistance and support for healing or resolution. This sort of collegial relationship among awakened teachers is rare and, we feel, highly desirable for the future of spiritual work in the world.

Our ethics policy

The teachers and mentors, as stated earlier, have agreed to comply with a policy that puts limits on teacher-student romantic or sexual involvement. This is not designed to prevent a potentially beautiful relationship from happening, but to help ensure that students in a vulnerable condition are not taken advantage of by those who are there to support them. The following will give you a taste of what our intentions are around this very loaded issue.

- Teachers/mentors will not engage in any sexual contact with participants during workshops or retreats.
- If there is a romantic interest between a teacher or mentor and a student, that student will be assisted in getting their feet on the ground and in finding another teacher to work with before the teacher or mentor opens a relationship consideration with them.
- Teachers or mentors who are serving a student in an ongoing primary relationship (doing private sessions on a regular basis) will not initiate any romantic or sexual contact with that student, nor respond to any overture by the student.
- If a sustained interest develops, and if both are free of other romantic commitments, there are steps to follow (including a three-month "cooling off" period) to make sure the student has established adequate support relationships before moving forward.
- In all cases, the goal is for all parties to be supported in ways that will help them navigate the especially volatile arena of romantic and sexual engagement. By participating in mutuality groups and being transparent with our feelings, our intention as conscious teachers is to help one another avoid the most significant lapses of judgment that can occur in private, one-on-one situations.

The arena of sexuality has been notorious for such lapses of good judgment and hypocrisy on the part of otherwise trusted and revered spiritual teachers, which is the reason our ethics policy focuses primarily on it. However, we are also mindful of the potential for abuse in the areas of money and power, and address these areas in our ethics policy as well. In regards to power issues and differentials, we are careful not to tell students what to do. You, and only you, are in charge of your life. Your teacher may make suggestions for things you might want to try; things they feel will facilitate your unfoldment and integration. And, of course, in many cases you will want to follow those suggestions in order to benefit from their experience—but you should always feel free to follow your own inner guidance. If your teacher ever makes demands on you that feel uncomfortable or unreasonable, please bring your concerns up with other members of your support team for a full review.

And the same basically applies in the arena of money. You do not have to purchase anything special, or get involved in any business schemes with any teacher in order to participate in this work. This teaching and support is available on a fee-for-time basis. Of course, there are workshops and retreats to attend (highly recommended!), and books and other resources available to purchase that will expand your understanding of divinely human awakening. But again, if you are ever asked to participate in anything that seems somehow "off" to you, feel free to discuss it with other members of your support team before signing on.

Tantric initiations

Another phenomenon of the embodied awakening process is that there may come a time when your whole being is consumed by a passionate, sexual desire for someone you have met along the path. This might be a teacher, a mentor, or a fellow student, and these sorts of eruptions are no respecter of socially-approved boundaries like marriage or committed relationships with other people. In this community, we informally refer to this phenomenon as "tantric initiations." They're "tantric" because they involve the dance of opposites, in this case the dance of sexual polarity, and they're "initiations" because they are almost always spiritually catalytic in nature.

It seems that tantric initiation is somehow related to the embodiment process itself, as the whole being is energized and opened to more refined currents of subtle energy. Such a high-intensity infatuation is quite compelling, so perhaps Being, in its own ingenious way, uses it to help bring your attention and identity-gravity fully down into your physical and emotional bodies. Whatever its divine purpose, there is no doubting its power and effectiveness in getting the attention of those who find themselves caught up in its thrall.

To make best use of this tantric fire, be sure to let your support team know what is happening with you, as they can help you sort out the threads of your feelings, navigate the potential pitfalls and complications, and support you in using this energy to further your embodiment process.

Since tantric initiations happen without regard for other relationships in your life—or in the life of the person you are feeling attracted to—it can be difficult to know what to do with this energy. The temptation to act it out and consummate the relationship can be quite strong, and it is only natural to feel fearful about what might happen to your current relationships. And while this sort of intense attraction can bring about the beginning of a life-altering relationship if both parties are available to take that on, often it is not actually about that. It may simply be there to help awaken you on multiple levels of your being. A tantric initiation does not mean that you need to leave your current relationship (if you're in one) and run off together—in fact this might be exactly the wrong thing to do. What is most beneficial, ultimately, is to sit within this fire—to burn with it—and let it alchemically transform you as it will.

While we celebrate the openings and sexual liberation that such initiations can bring, if you find yourself in the throes of such an initiation we also support you in staying in conscious communication, especially with your current partner (if any) who may feel threatened and confused by what's happening to his or her mate. Ultimately, tantric energies can be used to reinvigorate existing relationships just as well as to inaugurate new ones, and no one can predict which will be the better outcome for you.

If such a tantric initiation is occurring in regards to a Waking Down teacher or mentor, there are guidelines that the teacher/mentor will follow so that everyone involved is supported in reaching the best possible outcome.

Building your support system

To recap, in order to make the best use of the available support, we encourage you to develop, in your own time and way, a team consisting of a teacher, a mentor, some peers who are fellow travelers on the path, a therapist you can turn to for working through the really sticky parts, and a group to participate with. This may sound daunting, but much of it will develop organically and naturally as you participate in sittings, retreats, and other events. Even if you live some distance from any teacher or other peers, you can still participate by traveling to events when possible, and through participation by phone.

You may well find that your spiritual community becomes another family for you, of a more conscious sort than your original one. Having a family like this is highly supportive of a successful and complete awakening into your divinely human life—and provides a venue for practicing mutuality that you might not easily find anywhere else.

Like any family, this one won't be perfect and is sure to trigger your broken zones at times and cause you to gnash your teeth in frustration. But its members, by and large, will continue to lean in with you if you are willing to lean in with them.

In summary

Events are a great way to get to know what Waking Down in Mutuality is all about. Individual teachers and some regional groups sponsor events and retreats of various kinds, and the Institute of Awakened Mutuality conducts introductory and advanced-level events as well as longer retreats.

Teachers have years of experience and training and are especially valuable resources for helping your fulfill your potential. Each teacher is utterly unique, and, fortunately, there are a number of them for you to choose from. They can be found, with photos and bios and often other writings as well, on **wakingdown.org.**

Mentors are also listed on the same website, with photos and bios. Once you are working regularly with a teacher, you are encouraged to find a mentor for further support and more opportunity for mutuality.

Peers can be found by attending sittings, or by attending courses or retreats which are listed on the Waking Down website also. Do add your name to the master mailing list, so you will receive notices of upcoming events and other news of interest.

Groups can be local sittings or other mutuality groups where people in a local area decide to meet on a regular basis, with or without a teacher present. If there isn't one happening in your local area, you could start one yourself, or you might be able to join a group that meets by phone bridge (group conference call). Sometimes such groups will continue to meet after a workshop or retreat, or other opportunities for this form of participation may open up from time to time.

Licensed Therapists who are also deeply involved in Waking Down are listed on **wakingdown.org/contacts.** There are many others whose approach would also be considered compatible with this work, including teachers and mentors who have taken training in body-centered approaches but might not be licensed therapists (they will list this information on their bio page).

This chapter has given you some guidelines for finding and working with people whose life purpose includes helping you reach your goals for embodied awakening and transformation in this lifetime. This book can only give you pointers and a conceptual framework to help you understand the whole-being transformation that may well already be underway in you. By working with a personal guide who has travelled a similar path, your awakening process has the greatest likelihood of flowering into its full potential.

There's more to relating than having a teacher or support team. Enter mutuality. . .

8

MUTUALITY AND LOVE-TRUST

Our Story: In the environment of "mutuality," we became freer and more authentic in our expression, knowing that perfection was not required. We also remained accountable to one another, ever-ready to see, admit, and even embrace our limitations, and make amends when necessary.

What is mutuality?

Mutuality is the art of honoring one's true and total self while also making room for others to be doing the same. In this chapter we'll explore what that simple statement means in practice. Mutuality is one of those things that, "takes minutes to learn and a lifetime to master."

Mutuality involves honest speaking, deep listening, and the giving and receiving of feedback, with a tacit agreement to stay in communication and try to work out problems when things get difficult. Sometimes it involves agreeing to disagree, and finding a way to be heart-connected anyway. Mutuality is such a key element of embodied awakening that we call our collective work "Waking Down in Mutuality." It is the venue where our awakening divinely human nature has the opportunity to come fully forward as we learn how to interact more consciously with others who are also awakening. Eventually, what we learn about conscious relating with other divinely human beings can be carried into all our relationships.

The special power of mutuality groups

There is a special power in groups beyond what is available in one-on-one situations. In a group situation, you are able to hear what a variety of people are experiencing, and see them in their challenges and their triumphs. And, as trust grows, you may find yourself willing to let them see you in your own struggles to be fully here. Although you might feel shy at first, over time you may find it easier to speak your raw truth within a group than at home with your intimate partner or family members. In those one-on-one situations, a great deal rides on how the relationship is going, so conflicts are often fraught with pressure and difficulty. But in a group, you get to practice speaking your truth and making room for others to speak theirs, without so much on the line.

In Chapter 7, I introduced mutuality groups as one way to come together to explore awakening. You can practice mutuality in teacher-led groups, if you are fortunate enough to live near a teacher who is offering sittings. Or you might find (or start) a peer-based mutuality group—they're beginning to crop up in a variety of locations and even meeting through conference phone calls. Because it's important to create a safe-enough space for mutuality to grow, I have posted some guidelines for mutuality groups that can be found on my website, **divinelyhuman.com.**

Vulnerably speaking your truth

Honoring your true and total self begins with speaking your truth—giving voice to what is going on in your inner experience, including the full range of successes and failures, joys and sorrows, wounds you've received and injuries you've caused. It includes your visions and dreams for your life, your family, and the world. Mutuality is risking to speak what you might have formerly wanted to keep private. It means allowing others to see all of your many moods, whether they be creative and dynamic or reactive, unattractive, or downright "dysfunctional." It also means letting others know when you're upset, disappointed, pissed off, or feeling like you want to cut off from them.

Mutuality means speaking up even when you fear that what you are about to say might be unpopular. It means taking the risk that others will disagree with you, as well. It is through these bold moves that your most authentic self begins to discover its right to be *here* just as it is, without apology.

We are not advocating speaking indiscriminately, however. Mutuality is not about walking into your office Monday morning and telling your boss all the backed-up judgments that you've been suppressing. Especially when you are just getting started, you will want to choose appropriate venues to practice mutuality, those places where you feel welcomed and safe enough, and also trust that confidentiality will be honored.

Responsible communication

Mutuality attempts to find the balance between uninhibited expression and being unnecessarily hurtful to others. In that light, practitioners are advised to speak about their own experience, feelings, and reactions, and pay special attention to any urge to want to blame what they're feeling on another person. *It is never okay to insult people or address them in ways that demean their character.* On the other hand, you are welcome to let people know when something they have said or done has hurt your feelings, scared you, or brought up anger. The idea is to let people know how they have impacted you, knowing that your reaction is your own responsibility (and that someone else might have felt entirely differently about what was said or done). But if you don't let them know, they may well continue to do things that bring pain to you—so it is honoring both of yourself and the relationship to let them know how you are feeling so that adjustments, if necessary, can be made.

In the early stages when you are just learning how to GET here as your true and total self, don't worry too much about what other people might think. Most of us have adopted patterns of withholding our true feelings from others out of fear or shame. Just think about it: one of our most primal fears is that we will be shunned or cast out by our social community, because in our evolutionary past being cast out often spelled a certain death. We learn through a million subtle cues that 1) some others simply aren't interested in what we think and feel, 2) many others are uncomfortable talking about certain types of things, especially deep feelings, and 3) some types of thoughts and feelings are socially unacceptable and might cause us to be rejected, so it's better to keep them to ourselves.

To break out of the prison that these messages have put us in, we need to begin telling it like it is. It's more important to get it out than to have it be all polished and nice.

It's not just radical honesty

There's a difference, however, between mutuality and radical honesty. Mutuality is not simply about speaking the raw truth of whatever pops into your head at any given moment, without censorship. Nor does it mean pointing out others' bullshit bluntly, even when it is apparent to you, because this can overwhelm that person and lead them to distrust you. On the other hand, some sort of pointing out may be exactly what someone needs to hear in order to come out of a fog of self-deception. Mutuality flourishes in an environment of introspection, and willingness to discover the deeper truth behind your surface thoughts, reactions, and impulses. You might use this rule of thumb: begin by focusing on yourself and your own struggles to be in integrity and self-disclosure. If someone else seems out of integrity and you can't easily let it go, speak what is going on *in you* as you listen to them. Then you can be free of stewing about something, and they can take in what you have said to the degree possible for them in this moment. In this manner mutuality becomes a tool for self-discovery in relationship with others who are similarly motivated.

Mutuality takes into account the listener, staying mindful that they too are sensitive and vulnerable and will be impacted by what you say. Mutuality means speaking the difficult truth, but also sticking around to find out how your communication landed in the other person, and being willing to hear their feedback.

Active listening

The flip side of speaking about your own experience, feelings, and reactions is listening to others who are doing the same. Mutuality is very much a two-way street, where leaning in to listen as deeply and heart-fully as you can is just as important as stretching to speak your own truth.

Remember how a key element of the Inseeing Process is being able to bring the warm, interested curiosity of Presence to whatever is arising in you? That spacious welcoming is a powerful agent of healing, and it is this same sort of deep listening that is most beneficial in mutuality. To whatever degree you are capable in the moment, listen with whole-being openness, so that, if you had to, you could repeat back everything you have heard. Then reflect something back to the speaker, something that lets them know you heard them or empathically registered how they are feeling. It need not be the exact words (like you do when practicing Inseeing in pairs); a paraphrase is sufficient and more suited to the interpersonal dynamic of mutuality.

Being able to listen from Presence takes some practice. Typically, as we listen to someone speaking, we get activated ourselves and begin forming responses to what we're hearing even before the other person has finished speaking. If this happens, you can turn part of your awareness inward and say "hello" to whatever is coming up. Then return your full attention to the person who is speaking.

Speaking makes it (more) real

For humans, one of the ways we discover and confirm what is true for ourselves is through our words as we speak them to interested listeners. This is also and perhaps even more true when you are in a process of awakening and integrating your insights into your divinely human life. When given the opportunity to speak to conscious others who can understand, and validate, your experiences and new understandings, speaking your truth is very empowering and lends support for taking the steps that will bring you to a full and stable realization. It is natural to feel shy when you're speaking about the tender transitions that go with coming fully alive and awake, yet to find your voice in these tender places is the very thing that most helps your awakening become solid and trustable.

Unfortunately, cultural taboos can suppress speaking about spiritual awakenings. Some spiritual communities frown on it because it can stimulate jealousy in others or create competition around having the "best experiences" and "most progress." Or you may have heard something like, "He who knows does not speak"—as if talking about it somehow makes it less valid.

It's true that a profound awakening is a very personal experience that does not require—and can even be diminished by—speaking. For sure, it is better to hold one's tongue than to speak indiscriminately to people who have no framework from which to understand what you're saying, or to take it in the spirit in which it is intended.

For example, there were times in the past when someone who, following a profound mystical experience in which everything and everyone was seen to be of one divine essence, proclaimed, "I am God!" In the moment, that was the truth as they saw it. Unfortunately, such a statement could—and sometimes did—lead to persecution or even death. Whether we are conscious of it or not, our collective memories of such atrocities has led to a strong cultural inhibition against making statements that proclaim one's unity with "God."

In the western world at the beginning of the 21st century, we are very fortunate that we have great freedom to speak about our spiritual experiences with much less likelihood of being, for example, burned at the stake as witches. This is not to encourage being indiscriminate, but to definitely encourage leaning in and facing subconscious taboos in order to claim what is true for yourself. In the back and forth of mutual truth-telling, the most complete truth can be unearthed. And in stepping forward to tell your story, you support others in doing the same.

Speaking helps us see that we're not freaks, nor uniquely "bad"

There is another and very important benefit to be had by speaking your truth to others. If you hold back your private difficulties and embarrassments, you permit deep distortions to persist unchallenged. You may begin to believe that others are more together, successful, confident, capable, and happy than you are (indeed, you may *already* believe this to be true), and that something about you is more dysfunctional or broken than is true for other people. You may feel ashamed of the ways in which you think you fall short, or have failed to make your life work out as it should. While it's true that different people have different capacities and skills, and therefore some people are better at some things than others, it is a surprising discovery that almost everyone harbors a secret shame that they are somehow less than, or not as good as, others (even those who put on a good front and look really "together").

Such shame gives rise to a vicious circle: 1) you feel too ashamed to tell anyone the truth, and 2) your silence in turn reinforces your misconceptions about what it's really like to be human, and 3) your misconceptions lead to more shame and more silence.

When you speak up (in good company), you begin to undo this cycle. When you really get how difficult it is for *everyone* to be here, and how much embarrassment and shame everyone feels at times, you begin to release yourself from the demand to figure it all out and do it perfectly. You become free, and you set others free in the process.

"Coming out" is a service to others

Speaking can serve a special function in helping us *get here*— actually experience a radical shift into our divinely human embodiment. For human beings, verbal expression is one of our main ways of bringing things out of the realm of ideas and dreams into a shared field of reality. When we speak the discoveries and new perspectives that are arising in us, they get support to take root and grow.

In addition, it is easier to come into your spiritual maturity when you know there are others like you in the world. When you are engaged in a profound transformative process, you may feel as if you are changing so much that you will lose all your friends; that you and they will no longer be able to relate to each other in the same easy fashion that comes from sharing common frames of reference. There is some truth to this. Awakening precipitates shifts and changes in how you show up in your life as you become more authentic, and some of your former friends may drift away in the process if they aren't able to appreciate who you really are.

Most likely the people who love you will enjoy your growing authenticity, as well as the opportunity you create for them to express themselves more fully also. The good news is that, as you let people see who you are, you will draw new people into your life, people who *like* the real you! In our experience, new relationships always get formed with people who are attracted to, and resonate with, your true and total self.

You will not be alone in your awakeness. More and more people are now undergoing the radical shifts of spiritual awakening. But they—we—are still rare on planet earth, so whenever someone "comes out" and proclaims their awakened condition, they are rendering a service to the whole community. They are saying, in effect, "Come on in, the water's warm and you're going to find a whole new community of people who will recognize you and join you in exploring this new territory."

Balancing masculine and feminine

Speaking one's truth can also serve to bring the masculine and feminine sides of your nature into dynamic balance. The feminine side is where intuitions, feelings, values, and hurt places reside in our psyche. For most of us, this is our private world, the part of us that society teaches us to keep hidden or only share with our chosen inner circle. However, keeping this rich meaningful treasure trove hidden can also be disempowering, so that you end up living your public life in a sort of half-light.

The masculine side is the doing side, oriented to action, manifestation, and accomplishment. Although this side is socially acceptable, it can tend to run off half-cocked, as it were, if it is not informed by the feminine side so that it is taking action on the very things that really matter deeply to your authentic self.

Speaking your truth is where the two begin to work together. When the voice is used, the private world is brought out—made manifest—into the shared world. With practice and positive experience, confidence grows. When you discover that you are able to speak what you formerly felt was unspeakable, and that you are not rejected, discounted, or shunned, you begin to change and come alive in ways that you could never have predicted or imagined. Self-confidence and trust grow as you discover what is possible.

Mutuality puts all of our skills into use

In Chapter 5, Inseeing was defined as the experience of seeing into another living being so totally that it is as if you were standing in their center and understanding them from that perspective. You *insee* their wholeness and divine perfection, in and of itself, without needing to change it in any way. When you practice Inseeing, you become more able to *be* the spaciousness of Presence, which has room for all your conditioned parts, broken zones, and partial selves. Presence effortlessly holds all of the inner parts without needing them to change in any way. And then, almost magically, when parts are held in this unconditional fashion, they begin to spontaneously change and evolve into greater wholeness.

In mutuality, the process occurs a little differently. The speaker is more free to speak *as* whatever conditioned state or partial self is wanting attention, while the listener(s) take the role of Presence— to whatever degree is possible for them in the moment. There is a tacit understanding that the speaker is *more* than what he or she is expressing—that it's only one aspect of the totality of Who They Are (whether they currently are aware of that or not). This framework provides a context for mutual Inseeing: beholding the divinity of one another so fully, it's as if you were inside them, understanding them from that perspective. And having room for all that they are to be there, without needing to make any of it change.

Mutuality takes our inner work of self-discovery out into the interpersonal arena and shares it. It empowers everyone, not simply to become uninhibited about sharing personal information, but to become confident that we have a divine right to be here as we are, without shame. Through sharing we learn that our presence and our words matter to other people, and can help them heal and get here in all of their magnificence, too. When we open up together with the intention of becoming more fully conscious, we learn that our old ways of viewing things aren't the only possibility. As we take in more perspectives, we increase the likelihood of discovering deeper underlying truths—truths that transcend our personal stories.

Try this: Inseeing in mutuality

Here is a way to begin incorporating Inseeing into mutuality. When you are invited to share something about yourself, take a moment to pause and sense inwardly, into your core where you are most likely to get a felt sense of what's up for you right now— what might bring the greatest benefit by speaking it to good listeners. Say an inward "hello" to it, and then begin your sharing by saying, "I'm sensing something in me that _____." Fill in the blank with whatever you are in touch with—something that wants some attention, or maybe something that feels tense, or hurting, or even happy. Maybe it's something from the past that's triggered and would like some space to talk it through. It's not necessary to go through all the specific steps of the Inseeing Process at this time. Just let yourself spontaneously speak what's up, knowing that others are hearing you and holding you.

When you are the listener, you can sense how your body is registering what the other person is speaking. Sometimes you might feel a deep empathy with the other, and when you reflect what you are sensing back to the speaker, they will likely feel really "gotten" by you. However, there may be times when you feel triggered or reactive in light of what they're sharing. You might, at such times, place your hand over the area that is activated and inwardly greet it with a "hello, I see you there." And, often as not, that will give you enough breathing room to be able to return your attention to what the speaker is sharing. You might check if this "something in you" would like you to give it some dedicated attention later— and if so, be sure to do that.

"Wounds created in relationship are most deeply healed in, and by, relationship."

This statement, made by senior Waking Down teacher Sandra Glickman, reminds us that mutuality is one of our most powerful healing tools. Your interactions with others will sooner or later trigger your broken zones, and it is precisely *during* these times of regression into old feeling states that consciousness can penetrate into those dark places. Consciousness will bring new light, new insights, and new possibilities where before there was only the prospect of endless repetitions of the same patterns over and over. Healing begins when you re-experience a painful event, but in a different context than the original—for instance, while in the company of people who actually care about you and your feelings.

You then have the opportunity, in *this* moment, to form new conclusions about what's possible here in life.

Getting triggered into your old, conditioned patterns is not pleasant nor usually what you think you want. But it's a very valuable part of your process of becoming divinely human and able to participate in life with creative action rather than automatic reaction. As you open these areas up, consciousness can flow in, giving you new understanding and possibilities.

Mutual triggering

Given human nature and how difficult it is to really get a handle on everything going on inside yourself, it's inevitable that engaging with others is going to, at times, result in a messy situation. Despite your best intention to listen from a state of Presence, you'll find yourself flaring up into reactivity, triggered by what the other person is communicating. It might not even be what they actually said. Maybe they just reminded you of a situation from your past and *wham*, you're off and running with a whole pattern of upset. Then your reaction might trigger further reaction in the other person, and before you know it, there's a blowup replete with misunderstandings and hurt feelings. Now what?

Equalizing pressures

On an energetic level, when you feel injured by someone it is likely that they have sent out some energy, perhaps unintentionally, that you are reacting to. You may experience a complex mixture of anger, sadness, pain, agitation, etc. Or you may run through an inner litany of grievances and arguments as if on a tape loop, re-hashing the situation over and over or imagining ways to get back at the person, or to prove that you were right and they were wrong. When this is happening, you are *backed up* with this issue and may find it very difficult to let it go—or to have it let *you* go.

What is called for is a means of releasing and equalizing that pressure so you can return to a state of ease. If you are not conscious of this energetic dynamic, you may tend to hold high levels of pressure in your body because you don't know how to release it, or aren't even aware they're present. This can go on for years on end. Although there are many ways to release this energy—even enjoyable ones like lovemaking—the result of this mounting pressure is all-too-often an explosive outburst or attack directed at whoever happens to be handy when the dam breaks. The positive side of such outbursts is that you feel some relief. But the downside of this approach—and it's a significant one—is the collateral damage done if the pressure release comes as hostile, attacking energy. Now the next person is highly pressurized and will sooner or later need to blow *their* top to equalize their pressure. And so the cycle is perpetuated.

Another way you might try to release pressure is by turning your hostility inward, on yourself. While avoiding collateral damage to others, this can become quite crippling to your psyche and health.

Daring to speak

However, when you speak the difficult feelings you're backed up with to appropriate people in a constructive way, the energy can be released without the sort of major eruption that can damage a relationship. You may be judging yourself or attempting to censor your thoughts and not express them, but if they don't go away easily, you may have little choice but to give them voice. What doesn't get spoken will only fester and lead to other, less appropriate methods of expression. Or else it may contribute to an inner toxic environment that creates fallout of other kinds, like illness or depression. It's not healthy to hold the sorts of inner tension that we have come to take for granted in Western culture!

It's not easy to acknowledge your judgments and reactions and to bring them to another. You may feel embarrassed that you are having such thoughts, or even suspect that it's as much about you as it is about them. You may also feel reluctant to let them see your pain, or your vulnerability. But it is in these very places that seem so messy and difficult that amazing healing can occur, even healing of long-standing issues that you thought might live in you forever.

Staying in the room

For mutuality to really work there needs to be an agreement to stay in the room with each other long enough to hear feedback and work through the sticky parts. If someone says or does something that hurts your feelings, or pressures you, it is important to let them know, and take a stand for your own empowerment. Mutual interactions are seldom simple. What was it about what they said that got you so triggered? Perhaps their communication reminded you of something very hurtful that happened to you in the past. As you are sharing your reaction, you also have the opportunity to revisit that event and bring some healing to it.

This is not to say that all reactions are solely the responsibility of the one experiencing them. That would be going too far. Mutuality is a messy process where all sides play a part in working together to explore and learn from the broken zones and conditioned responses that inevitably get triggered when people interact. It is impossible to totally avoid this sort of inadvertent hurt that happens in relating, because no one can know where another's broken zones lie. And most people aren't fully aware of where their own broken zones lie, never mind other people's broken zones. In relationship, you will likely find yourself repeatedly surprised by the intensity of some of your reactions to even innocuous comments or situations, and whenever that happens, you will have to work your way carefully through the fallout in order to come to a positive resolution and a restoration of harmony and trust.

Staying present does NOT mean taking abuse

Staying in the room, however, doesn't mean allowing yourself to be abused. Abuse is never useful, and allowing it to continue harms not only the receiver, but the abuser as well, and has devastating consequences on relationship. Constructive learning and growth cannot happen in that kind of environment. It is neither desirable nor suggested that anyone should passively allow others to be abusive toward them, whether the abuse is overt and physical, or subtle and verbal. It is part of taking responsibility for everyone's wellbeing to walk away if someone demeans you, calls you names, insults you, or threatens your safety in any way.

Much abusive behavior is unconscious, so those who have been abusive need to bring their behavior into conscious awareness in order to modify it. It is best for them (and their friends and loved ones) if they will seek professional help and guidance with this. In the meantime, those who love them can help by *leaving the situation when abuse begins*, and only returning when the abusive party is able to be present without resorting to that sort of inappropriate communication.

For people who have a history of abuse as children, or who've been caught up in a chronically-abusive relationship, it may be difficult to distinguish what is abusive or to know when to walk away. Some people don't even know that there are other ways to communicate that aren't abusive. If you are unsure about how to draw the line, please talk to a skilled counselor who can help you learn how to create healthy boundaries.

So how do you distinguish what is abusive? Anger in and of itself is not abusive. It becomes abusive when it resorts to insults, name-calling, demeaning remarks designed to hurt your self-esteem, or tactics intended to prevent you from expressing yourself. Physical threats or attack are also abusive. You never need to remain with someone who is engaging in this sort of behavior.

In most cases, the conversation can be resumed once the triggered person has calmed down and become civil. However, if you don't feel safe enough to continue one-on-one, you may need to bring in a third party to mediate so that a trustable environment can be maintained.

When to use a third party (when really triggered)

Given how challenging mutuality can be, no one is expected to do it perfectly. That's part of the gift that we can give one another: understanding that we won't be able to always do it "right" or "nicely" or avoid pushing each others' buttons.

Although we do recommend speaking directly to one another and staying in the room to work things through, there are also times when it will be best to bring your feelings to a third party first, especially when you are highly triggered. If you find yourself so angry or distraught that you want to attack the other person, and take their head off or say things that insult their character, it is advisable to turn to a trusted helper and ask them to hear you out. In that fashion some of the pressure can be released and you can sort through the waves of feeling that might be coming very fast at that moment. Then you will be able to make a more informed choice about whether, and how much, to bring to the person who triggered your reaction in the first place.

Using a third party in the form of an awakened therapist (or teacher), is also strongly recommended when you are feeling chaotic inside, when your emotions threaten to overwhelm you, or when you find yourself struggling to understand what is arising in you internally. Therapists are trained to give you their undivided attention in order to help you sort through things and gain insight and healing. Most of us at one time or another need this sort of assistance in order to work our way through past traumas and gain some freedom around them. Mutuality may be too challenging when you are dealing with major interpersonal crises, but the personal work you do during those times will give you a foundation for even deeper mutuality going forward.

Mutuality with WDM teachers

Sometimes it might be your teacher who pushes your buttons. Teachers make mistakes, react inappropriately at times, create messes in their personal relationships, do things that they wished later they hadn't done, etc. Sooner or later, your teacher may disappoint you (especially if you were idealizing them in some fashion). If you find yourself feeling hurt by something your teacher has said or done, or not said or done, it is your opportunity to practice YOUR end of mutuality and let them know.

Mutuality outside WDM

Mutuality, in the sense of having the intention to stay in communication and work things through even when it gets difficult and messy, is best practiced with others who have agreed to it. You cannot require it of anyone, nor force a reluctant person to meet you in that way. It is best by invitation, and by education. It will be easier for your loved ones to join you if they understand that your intention is to be healed, whole, and fully expressed in your life, and that you wish the same for them. If they remain uninterested, that is their choice to make. However, that does not prevent you from being honest in your communication with them. It is only through honest, direct communication that you can be free.

Not a utopian ideal

Mutuality is not some utopian ideal of the perfect community of people who are always loving, patient, and kind with one another. Or, perhaps I should say it's not a place where everyone is always "nice." In fact, "nice" is one of those concepts that tends to keep people suppressed and repressed. People who are trying to be nice adjust themselves to a perceived social standard to such an extent that they lose touch with themselves and what they really feel, want, and are willing to take a stand for. In order to be fully here as an embodied divinely human person, this tendency to suppress oneself has to be reversed, whatever it takes. Mutuality is the sort of real, intimate, and honest mutual engagement that can help further our collective unfoldment into our full potential. It's challenging and sometimes messy. It can be a real workout!

Love-trust

We have all experienced things in our lives that caused us to begin distrusting others. Because humans are not perfectly attuned and sensitive to one another, it is inevitable that they will sooner or later do something that hurts another. And given human nature, this can run the gamut from completely unintentional to downright vicious intentional harm. It would be foolish for us to ignore this fact about humans: we can be mean to one another, and we've all experienced that at one time or another in our lives.

In light of this, it is pretty remarkable that people can be trusting at all. Trust is a precious commodity, something that allows us to let down our guard around another and allow them to see our tender side. Trust is a gift—it says to another, "I am willing to take a chance with you, to let you get close to me with the assumption that you won't mistreat me if I do."

For healthy people, trust with someone new develops in stages, organically, over a period of time. First there are small intimacies, invitations that let the new person know something personal about us. If this is met with care and not used against us, there can be greater intimacies and deeper sharing. If this is respected then we move to greater intimacy, perhaps including physical intimacy, and only if this level is handled well do we consider taking further steps—like living together, or forming a business partnership, or getting married.

Growing trust

Of course, no one is perfectly considerate all the time—we are far too preoccupied with just trying to make it through our own lives to always take our friends' and lovers' interests into account. There will be missteps along the way—but a big part of establishing healthy, trusting relationships is what happens after things get messy.

If a friend or partner acts inconsiderately, then is unwilling to listen to you when you bring your grievance to them, you will naturally feel that your trust has been misplaced with this person and that it is unsafe to continue being vulnerable around them. On the other hand, if they do listen respectfully, and let you know what's going on in them as well as expressing sincere regret for the hurt you feel, then trust can actually deepen as a result of such breaches.

This dynamic of gradually building trust with another over time does not come easily to everyone. Children raised in abusive situations—no matter if the abuse is physical, verbal, or sexual, or whether it is invasive or by omission—may have such deep wounding in the area of trust that they simply don't know what trust is, never mind how to achieve it.

Blind trust

If you didn't have the process of gradually building trust over time modeled for you, you may either distrust everyone, or you might be overly-trusting with people you don't know very well. Blind trust is practically a given in romantic stories: when the handsome or beautiful stranger appears, all caution is thrown to the wind as you give yourself over completely to the fantasy that this person will never betray or cause harm, and that you will live happily ever after. Taking the time to build trust gradually may be viewed as decidedly un-romantic and therefore its value can be overlooked.

Many people seem especially prone to blind trust of religious or spiritual teachers. Shouldn't they be safe people to trust, since they say they're committed to living by a higher standard than the average person? But you only have to listen to the spiritual grapevine a while to realize that more than a few highly respected spiritual figures have fallen ignominiously from grace and misused the position of trust they were given.

Blind trust sees things only in black-and-white, and when the inevitable letdowns occur, there is shock and outrage in response. Blind trust says, in effect, "I know you'll never hurt me because you are a good person." Blind trust completely ignores the fact that no one is perfect, or capable of always having your best interests in mind (even if they do have them at heart). Blind trust is a setup for being disappointed. When you've been overly trusting, you are unlikely to weather the inevitable ups and downs that occur between real people in real relationships.

Pragmatic trust, on the other hand, is healthier. It says, in effect, "I am hopeful that you won't hurt me intentionally, although you might accidentally. I'll hang around and see how you show up over time." This sort of conditional trust allows a relationship to go forward, step by step, as both parties get to know the other's style of relating and their trustworthiness.

Trust is also an inside job

Trust is not just about how the other person treats you. It is also about how well you trust yourself to land on your feet in dynamic interactions with others. As you grow in your ability to be in Presence with all your feelings and emotions, you will feel more confident of your ability to embrace what gets triggered in you by the behavior of others around you. This is not to say you will welcome callous treatment by others, but that you will be able to extend more trust to those around you if you trust yourself enough to know they will not be able to damage or destroy you by what they say or do.

The art of being accountable

Saniel Bonder has been a powerful teacher for me, in a number of areas. Not the least was through the way he coura-geously pioneered a profound spiritual work (Waking Down in Mutuality) while simultaneously being a flawed, imperfect human being. Of course, we ALL are flawed and imperfect, but Saniel demonstrated how someone could embody a profound spiritual understanding yet not be a saint (a perfectly compassionate, patient, and understanding spiritual guide).

Saniel has a fierce, fiery side that, at times, flares up without warning. And he has taken flak for that. Unlike teachers and leaders who keep their reactivity out of the spotlight when in front of a group, Saniel chose not to hide his reactivity. And that was pretty challenging: it required those around him to confront the predicament of "perfect imperfection." It became a profound teaching.

See, no one can ever know if they have fully plumbed the depths of all their unconscious broken zones, nor can they fully know that they won't fall into a conditioned or trance state and begin acting unconsciously in their relationships from time to time. Whether for a brief period or a more protracted phase, "unconscious" is just that—out of sight, beneath awareness. It only becomes *conscious* when there is reflection from others to help reveal what's going on. Any unconscious pattern will only cease to drive our behavior when it has been fully seen and worked through over time.

Unfortunately, spiritual awakening does not immediately change your ingrained patterning. This is what mystifies so many people: why doesn't a profound revelation of your divinity immediately do away with fear and its resultant survival strategies, or with selfishness, or with unkind behavior to others? The answer has to do with how you are wired: your survival patterns (and most of your patterns are somehow linked to your sense of safety) are necessary and therefore quite resistant to change. So the predicament you'll face as an awakening, divinely human being is that, while on some level you'll have transcended feeling alone in the universe, or cut off from Source or divine love, you will still be conditioned to act in ways that are quite different than you might expect from an awakened person. Or prefer.

But our human nature isn't second class to our divine nature—it is actually *also* divine. The broken, wounded, childish one crying out in outraged fury is every bit as divine as the sublimely peaceful one who is embodying grace in the moment. Unconscious doesn't mean un-divine. This is a really important point worthy of deep contemplation. Most of us automatically assume that "divine" means "of the light"—all that is good, flowing, loving, compassionate, creative, joyful, or wise. And we assume that the ways in which we are conditioned, reactive, self-protective, egoic, angry, resistant, etc., are not of the light. We judge ourselves and others by this yardstick, looking in vain for that which embodies all light and no dark, all love and no fear, all good and no bad, or all freedom and no limitation.

Even when we accept conceptually that we are ALL of the entire range of experience and response, and accept that awakened people also continue to embody the entire range of human behavior, on some level we may hold out hope for a type of virtue that is still very rare on earth. And we may continue to hold a dualistic view that judges people as "less divine" if they demonstrate personal weaknesses, vulnerability, or reactivity. It is worth looking at—these ways we hang onto our hopes and expectations, for ourselves and others, that we and/or they will become totally safe and trustable, so that we won't have to feel so scared any more.

Well, in the early '90's when I spent a lot of time around Saniel, he wasn't always as "safe" as folks around him would have liked. While some people found his heat quite enlivening, others found themselves triggered and shaken deep in their bodies. Some spiritual teachers would have shielded themselves from criticism behind a position like: "It's the divine right of awakened beings to behave any way they wish and they shouldn't be questioned by their students. If you have a problem, there's something wrong in you and you should work on that." But Saniel took a different approach, and modeled for us a way to honorably deal with the fallout that comes from the inevitable messiness of human relationships. He called it "coconut yoga."

Coconut yoga

Coconut yoga is a rather whimsical term that means to bow down to the aggrieved party, as if your head were falling to the ground like a coconut dropping from a tree—with a big THUNK. In short, this means being willing to receive people's feedback when they feel hurt or wronged by you, and to make a real apology that indicates your concern and interest in not repeating that kind of injury.

Showing up to receive feedback in this manner is not often easy or fun—that's why it's called "yoga." It is a spiritual practice, and it takes practice to develop some facility with it. Most of us have a knee-jerk reaction to critical feedback that instantly goes to avoidance, denial, or defense. We either don't want to take responsibility for our accuser's pain, or we want to turn it back on them and make them see how they caused us to act that way. It's difficult to just sit and let the feedback in—but that is what is needed to begin to undo the cycle of injury, blaming, and defensiveness that causes people to withdraw from one another in distrust and hurt feelings.

And this is what Saniel was somehow able to do. He would invite the feedback, listen respectfully, and make sure he really understood how the injured party was registering the situation. And then he was (almost always) able to feel and express his compassion for their sense of injury, and his remorse. Even if the complaint felt unwarranted or unfair, or was clearly the result of that party's own broken zones or unreasonable expectations, Saniel would do his best to find his part of the responsibility, own it, and offer to make amends.

Coconut yoga doesn't instantly erase the soreness that can result when you feel missed, or mistreated, by someone else, but it usually clears the way for healing to begin. While not perfect, it may well be the best skill we can learn to foster true healing between people. Unlike the typical drama of relationship, where hurt feelings either escalate into full-blown fighting (with attacking and greater injury) or cause withdrawal into icy silence, this is a third option with the potential to defuse the situation and initiate a process of healing.

Over the years, due to his sustained attention and much help from his friends, colleagues, and students, Saniel took much greater responsibility for his tendency to flare up without warning, so that people rarely encounter him that way anymore. If he feels the impulse to express some intensity, he is more able to let people know it's coming—thus lessening the impact—and then debrief with them immediately afterward. This is a great example of how sustained mutuality can rub off the rough edges of a person's reactivity, thus fostering ever-greater intimacy and love-trust.

Forgiveness—the final piece

There's a lot said in many spiritual teachings about forgiveness. We are told that the loving thing to do is forgive, and that forgiving is good for us. But just as blind trust is unwise, blind or too-quick forgiveness can be counter-productive to genuine healing between people. You may have good reasons NOT to forgive that person, at least not yet.

Forgiving someone as a spiritual practice may feel good and virtuous, but if you haven't really allowed yourself to feel and process the full extent of the impact that person's behavior has had on you, it may be a superficial act that doesn't really release the trauma. Your best intentions to let go of a grievance may not be able to get much traction if the grievance won't let *you* go.

One reason for holding onto a grievance can occur when something in you is trying to keep you from being hurt again. You might think that forgiving means acting as if the injury never happened, or that you need to open yourself to this person again. However, forgiving someone *doesn't mean you now have to blindly trust them again*, or allow them the same access to your tender inner parts. That MAY be the outcome, but depending on the degree of impact they have had on you, and the degree to which they broke your trust, you may need to create some new boundaries between you. With time, and depending on your mutual motivation to rebuild your relationship, trust can be gradually rebuilt if you both work toward that end.

Once you realize that you can forgive someone without re-engaging at the same level of intimacy, it becomes easier to at least have a willingness to forgive. The actual forgiveness, when the charge is fully dissipated, comes when it does, more an act of grace than of will. After all, the more honest we are with ourselves, the more we see that we all share a common human predicament. We mess up. We make mistakes. Sometimes we hurt one another. Sometimes we just fail to see how we're impacting others through our actions or our neglect. Forgiveness is a generous act; it's compassion in action. When we extend forgiveness we are making it easier for all of us to be here as our flawed human selves.

All that said, if you haven't yet expressed your hurt feelings to the one who triggered them, you may simply be unable to let it go. The hurt may cycle around in your thoughts and/or emotions without any means of resolution until it is spoken in an appropriate fashion—and received by the other person. To that end, here are some guidelines to follow if you find yourself in a situation that calls for making amends.

Coconut yoga guidelines

A) Bringing feedback

- If you are the person bringing the complaint, do your best to speak about your experience and your feelings or reactions without making the other person solely responsible for creating these feelings in you. Your feelings are your own. The other person's actions or words may have triggered them, but your reaction is uniquely your own and may well have as much to do with what happened to you in the past as it does the current situation. It's not, however, necessary to figure all that out in advance—give yourself permission to be imperfect in your presentation.

- Have an idea of what you want to get out of the meeting. What will satisfy you? You may not get everything you want, but having some clarity around that will make it more possible for the other person to give it to you.

- Keep in mind that it's hard for most people to hear feedback, especially those who had critical parents and for whom criticism brings forth extreme shame. Try to make some allowance for them to be imperfect at this, too.

- Try to be *willing* to forgive the other for whatever they did that brought you pain.

B) Receiving feedback

- To whatever degree you can, stay open to receiving feedback from anyone who registers that they are feeling hurt or wounded by you in some way. Keep in mind how difficult it is for people to come forward with their feedback and try to support them in their effort.

- Practice active listening by repeating the essence of what you have heard them say. Continue until they agree that you have fully gotten their message. Do this before you jump in and present your side of the issue.

- Find in yourself some sense of compassion or regret for the hurt they feel, even if you don't think you caused it or should be held responsible. Let them know you care about how they feel. If you can't feel compassion for their pain or upset, it is a clue that you might be feeling defensive or unjustly accused. Rather than fake it, let them know in the simplest way possible that you're not fully available to meet them at this time. Plan another meeting.

- If you felt too triggered to go forward, talk to a teacher or other member(s) of your support team and explore what has come up in you around the incident.

- If the situation feels highly pressured, you might ask someone to join you and act as a mediator when you next meet. Sometimes both sides want to have a support person present.

- Find out what the person bringing feedback wants from you, either an apology or some other form of amends. If possible, give them what they want, including your sincere intention to not repeat the same behavior in the future.

- Check in and see if she or he is willing to hear your side of the issue, if not now then at some time in the near future when you could meet again.

Remember that coconut yoga is a generous gesture towards mutuality rather than something anyone is entitled to receive. It is a gift when someone is willing to participate in this fashion, so try to appreciate their efforts even if not done perfectly. Coconut yoga is as much about the empowerment you get from daring to bring your feedback—and then being seen and heard by the other—as it is about anything specific that they say or do in response. If you remember that your old wounds were often compounded by the fact that no one was available to see and hold you in your pain, you will realize what a great healing gift we extend to one another when we are willing to listen and honor.

If your attempt at coconut yoga goes wrong, as it sometimes will, and things seem to be getting worse than when you began, *ask for assistance*. There are many people in the Waking Down community who will lean in with you to help bring about a positive resolution.

Awakened community

I've written extensively here about the challenges of relating in mutuality. And although I have described some of the benefits that come from being freely expressed (i.e., speaking your truth), this chapter would be incomplete if I didn't at least attempt to convey the real heart of mutuality, the payoff of all the hard work.

Mutuality creates the container for Being to see and encounter Being, deeply, fully, even passionately. As people awaken, at least when it's an embodied awakening, they come ever more fully into their unique expression. They become more independent and autonomous the more they take responsibility for their own lives. They also become more willing to state their opinions even when they might be unpopular, and one effect of all this is that they become far less likely to just "go along to get along." While they become more open to hearing others' viewpoints, they also become less willing to give up their own to make someone else comfortable. In other words, a room full of divinely human beings is likely to be a room full of strong personalities who love deeply yet aren't afraid to mix it up from time to time.

Awakening Being seems to somehow thrive on just such encounters. It's as if the light that shines out of my eyes gets excited whenever it sees a similar light shining out of other eyes, and just wants to hang out with "itself" appearing as the "other" over there. The fact that each unique person comes with a personality is just the way it is, and it's the nature of the beast for personalities to bump up against one another about as often as they fall into synergistic harmony. In the very bumping up against, we bring to light the ways we aren't yet as understanding or compassionate as we wish to be, and thus create opportunities for deeply healing our broken zones. This in turn leads to greater freedom and greater room for divine Self-expression. We call forth the divine in one another by our willingness to see and be seen, hear and be heard, meet and be met.

Mutuality begins with an intention to hang out together for our mutual growth and benefit, and it really matures when conflicts arise and get successfully sorted out through a mutual intention to honor ourselves and one another as fully as humanly possible. We stretch our capacity to hold the inevitable tensions of human relatedness, and we become more trusting of ourselves, one another, and Being in the process. What we learn in mutuality groups then also extends into our other relationships outside the circle as well. We become more able to see, honor, and call forth the divine in every other being we encounter—whether they see it in themselves or not.

But there is no substitute for the company of other awakened and awakening people who can fully *get* you in all the dimensions of your total being. Being seen and recognized by those who relate to what you're experiencing validates and greenlights your tender awakening self to keep going toward ever-more-complete realization of its potential as a divinely human being.

What this is all leading to is awakening

Despite the psychological tone of this chapter, mutuality is not just a psychological program leading to mental health and wellness. It is a profound spiritual practice that creates a framework into which consciousness can fully arrive and find expression. Mutuality is both a practice that helps facilitate embodied awakening and also a means of giving expression to that awakening once it has occurred.

Not only does mutuality support and enhance embodied awakenings, awakening, in turn, is a prerequisite for the full flowering of mutuality in which the Other is seen to also be Self. It is only when you fully arrive in your divinely human awakening that you will be able to show up sufficiently to really engage mutuality full out. And so, with that in mind, let us move on to our next chapter, *Illuminations.*

9

ILLUMINATIONS

Our Story: Through gazing, transmission, meditation, or Inseeing, we became receptive to—and experienced—profound spiritual openings, compassion, and great love. We chose whatever forms of inquiry or practice we found most appropriate to support different phases of our unfoldment, as we discovered that peak experiences gave us valuable new perspectives yet were not the same as stable embodied awakening.

How to talk about the divine?

In this chapter I will more directly address the topic of awakening—the manner in which you begin to know the divine and experience yourself as an integral part of that Mystery. To do so, I need to find a way to describe something that is fundamentally unspeakable, and beyond our everyday experience.

It is remarkably difficult to speak about Consciousness, because Consciousness is not a thing or a process—and most of our language is used to describe objects or processes. We don't have many words in the English language to describe the ultimate Mystery (unlike the Sanskrit language, for instance, which has many words to describe the variety of spiritual experiences, openings, and understandings). The one English word that has been used a great deal in the past—"God"—has so many interpretations as to render it practically meaningless. For many current spiritual seekers, this word has lost its ability to stir them with wonder and awe.

But then, being human, we continue to try to find a means of talking with others about our discoveries and experiences, and about our *knowing*. If I were speaking with you personally, I would try to find out which words and frameworks have personal meaning for you and use them. For this writing, I will use a variety of words all pointing to the One Mystery which cannot, ultimately, be spoken. When I am referring to the universal, transcendent quality of a familiar word, I will capitalize that word to distinguish it from everyday meanings of the same word. As you read, feel free to translate my language into words that are more personally meaningful to you.

No amount of descriptive terms can convey the ultimate Mystery in a way that your rational, logical mind will understand. It's simply beyond the mind's scope. This is an important point— no matter how much you struggle to grasp the concept of awakening with your mind, you will fail. At some point you're going to look back and say that it's not what you expected! Still, we can try to create a framework with words, a framework that might serve to orient you toward something that will at some point become real for you, beyond words and concepts. If my attempt to describe the territory of awakening does nothing other than support and encourage you to hang in as your process unfolds, it will have served a useful purpose. Once you *know*, you *know*. You are changed by your discovery. New qualities become available to you, and you may find yourself communicating with others who *know* by a glance or a smile instead of speaking, sharing an understanding that is beyond words.

Whether or not you are aware of anything in you that transcends ordinary waking consciousness, I posit that you do have at least an *intuition* that you are something more. It is this very intuition that forms one side, so to speak, of the core wound which is where your limited, finite nature intersects with your infinite, divine nature. We all have within us the potential to become fully aware of our emerging divinity. In these next chapters, I will be speaking to that part of you that can understand beyond words, that already knows this information and is even now in the process of becoming more fully known and lived by you.

Peak experiences and glimpses

A glimpse or other unexpected peak experience can bring with it a wonderful new perspective on reality, and can occur to anyone at any stage of development. Most people will get at least a taste of *something more* at some point in their lives. It's not unusual to have a profound experience during childhood or adolescence, as if a veil has lifted and something very powerful and compelling breaks through, whether for a brief moment or for a longer time. A deeper sense of the nature of existence is revealed.

> *For example, when I was about five, I wandered from my home and discovered a pair of sunflowers growing by the side of a driveway. As I gazed up at the golden disks, they became the radiant "faces" of two beings that showered me with the most pure, unconditional love and acceptance I had ever felt. As I tell this tale, I know it would be easy to ascribe seeing faces in sunflowers as just a child's imagination, but there was something so real and true about the experience that it remains with me to this day, some 50 years later. Some bridge between physical reality and the transcendent dimension was opened for me on that day. It took nearly 30 more years before I was able to consciously reopen that bridge—but that early childhood experience was enough to convince me that there was more to life than my parents were teaching me.*

We may refer to these openings as peak experiences—a period of time in which the challenges and struggles of daily life shift into the background and the beauty and perfection of the transcendent dimension shines through, permeating us with its radiance. Or you might have an experience of being more fully, vibrantly embodied than ever before. Whether flashy and "cosmic," or a more subtle shift of perception, such experiences typically leave you *knowing* that all is right with the world, and with you, and with every aspect of your petty little life. You see how everything is inherently interconnected and whole. Truth perceived in this manner is self-validating, in the sense that you just *know* it's more true than anything else you've experienced in life to date. This kind of enhanced perception shifts concepts like "all is One" or "I am God" or "love is the only reality" from mere mental abstraction into lived experience—they become true for you as never before. And, even though the experience later fades away leaving you with only a memory, something in you gets permanently changed by a direct experience of this over-arching intelligence and perfection.

The awakening process

As discussed in Chapter 1, embodied awakening typically begins with a glimpse of a more expanded or transcendent perspective, which leads in time (perhaps years later) to questioning and rotting out of previously-held frameworks. As the unfolding progresses, a period of oscillating in and out of more expansive *states* is followed by a permanent shift into the new *stage* which is a paradoxical blend of transcendent and immanent, divine and human.

In this chapter I will explore illuminations and oscillations, in Chapter 10 I'll discuss the shift into irrevocable embodied awakening, and in Chapter 11 I'll say more about the integration process that follows such a shift.

Cultivating glimpses

Something deep in the human heart longs to taste the holy nectar of the divine, to reconnect with its Source or essence in a way that satisfies its restless seeking, that brings a sense of wholeness, completion, or relief from existential separateness or confusion. It's not unusual for someone to have a profound, perspective-altering experience that's followed by a long dry spell. Still, the experience remains as an anchor, or a touchstone, that draws them into a more serious exploration at some time later in life, when they begin to ponder the deeper questions of existence in hopes of regaining the state of spaciousness, flow, clarity, or bliss they once touched, that felt so right and true and full of meaning.

Such peak experiences, or revelations, always come by grace—according to divine timing rather than human desire or control. They typically come at the most unexpected moments. While mind-blowing experiences are not essential for the realization of your divinely human potential, a glimpse into a more transcendent framework can be deeply fulfilling, and it often motivates the ongoing search for a more lasting realization.

Although you cannot control the timing of such a glimpse, there are things you can do to increase the likelihood of experiencing something beyond ordinary reality. If you compare a glimpse to a breeze stirred by a divine hand, you will understand that you cannot force the breeze to come when you want it. However, you will have a greater chance of feeling it, as it were, if you are standing beside an open window.

Cultivation opens the window and places you beside it. There are lots of practices designed to cultivate spiritual experiences or insights, including: sitting quietly in contemplation; walking or sitting receptively in nature's beauty; prayer and invocations; ritual; devotional singing; shamanic journeying; expressions of appreciation and gratitude; reading or listening to inspiring pieces; contemplating "who am I" or other koans; attending sittings or satsangs (associating with awakened teachers); breathwork techniques; and more. Throughout the ages, people have turned to psychotropic substances, as well, to elicit mystical experiences and visions.

Four practices

Becoming divinely human, however, is not about having a different, more refined, or more transcendent view of things. Nor is it about achieving some kind of permanent residency in an expanded state of awareness. Embodied awakenings are inclusive by nature, and may not have the same kind of flashy experiences as some other paths generate. In evolutionary terms, it seems as if Consciousness has evolved its capacity for Self-exploration so that it no longer requires transcendence of the personal self in order to become Self-aware. The felt sense of the *embodied* Conscious nature will often be more grounded, and more richly textured, than descriptions of transcendent Consciousness. Yet it still includes a fundamental ease, or wellness of Being, as its basis.

While not technically required for embodied awakening, periods of illumination, insight, or blazes of Consciousness are useful adjuncts to the awakening process, whether they come before or after the fundamental shift into divinely human embodiment. If you are deep in "the rot," you may not be inclined to do much of anything that calls for effort, or takes you away from the pain of life, including trying to meditate or otherwise alter your state of awareness. That's really okay—there will be times for striving and times for simply being as you are, and both are natural and appropriate as you move through your awakening process.

During the darkness before dawn, the most useful supportive practices are often simply gazing and receiving of transmission, which I've written about at some length in Chapter 2. When you find yourself available for some cultivation, you may wish to explore meditation and/or Inseeing as supportive practices for opening your channels to the divine.

Meditation is a time-honored means of helping people get beyond their ordinary habits of mind in order to discover other aspects of their total nature. There are many types of meditation that lead to a variety of experiences including, but not limited to, insight into the habitual, repetitive nature of the thinking mind, or the quieting of mental activity altogether leading to a deep inner stillness. Although not essential, it might be easier for you to become aware of your true nature as Being, or Consciousness, when your mind is less active and intrusive. When your mind is running full tilt, you may be so identified with that thought stream that nothing else enters in. When thinking and the heart rate slow down, and the body becomes quieter, gaps in thought can occur that give you an opportunity to notice that you have an existence beyond thought. In this way, meditation is one of the best tools for discovering what lies beyond the parameters of your normal thinking mind. You don't have to take this on faith—it is something to investigate, avidly, to find whether it is indeed true for you.

There is no one "right" form of meditation for all people, because people vary so greatly. Initially, meditation may seem difficult and unnatural, because sitting still can heighten your awareness of your almost-obsessive thinking. But when you find the practice that resonates with you, you will likely find it to be easy, relaxing, and deeply nurturing—a great opportunity to rest deeply, recharge your batteries, and partake of a special sweetness that you normally overlook in the course of a busy day.

Once in a while, you may find yourself graced by the sense of a divine Presence, which can come as inner light, a sense of being filled with wondrous energy, being suffused with exquisite love or compassion, or of having your boundaries dissolve such that you feel yourself extending out into the far reaches of the universe. Or this Presence may come in the form of a divine being, deity, or avatar—such as Jesus, Krishna, Kwan Yin, or Mary. Or you may have a sense of contact with a spirit guide in human, animal, or other-worldly form. These types of contacts bring gifts, whether we know the nature of the gift at first or not. At the very least, they help us discover that creation is far more vast than our ordinary human lives normally reveal.

What begins as a deliberate practice of meditation (which involves some effort) will at some point evolve into effortless *deep contemplation.* Deep contemplation (which I am distinguishing from the more common sense of "contemplation" as thinking about or ruminating on a topic) happens when the essence of awakening Being (Presence) turns in upon itself rather than being turned outward toward the world. In contemplation you may feel yourself suffused with any of the qualities of the divine—clarity, peace, insight, effulgent light, divine love, inner strength, wisdom, fullness, emptiness, etc.—or you may simply *be.* Contemplation happens without any effort, as if you are simply settling down into who you are in your deepest essence and not striving for anything at all. The Buddhists call this *non-doing,* and it is one of the key doorways into the awakened life. It is also a means of savoring and deepening in whatever realization you are currently experiencing.

Some cautions about meditation

Some spiritual teachers emphasize the need for attaining a state of greater perfection in order to be worthy of grace. If you have been trying to use meditation as a tool to fix yourself or make yourself different or better than you already are, your meditation practice itself may have become an obstacle to your awakening. Or you might have come to assume that your true and total Self is only accessible during your periods of meditation, and not during the other hours of the day, and in this way be inadvertently limiting yourself. In either case, it may be useful to suspend your meditation practice for a while in order to discover what is effortlessly true in every moment of your experience. This is not an indictment of meditation, only a caution that it can sometimes create interference or a set of expectations that can get in the way of fully landing in 24/7 embodied awakening.

Another type of meditation that is potentially harmful is the practice of noticing everything that arises and then dismissing it by calling it "not me." While a version of this technique can be very useful in making a distinction between Awareness and its objects, this practice can exacerbate the dissociation people feel around disowned shadow aspects of their psyche, by reinforcing that they're "not me." Because I have found embodied awakening to be most supported by the radical embrace of ALL aspects of yourself, including the shadow parts that were formerly unwelcome, I recommend you steer clear of practices that are dissociative by nature.

Does the mind have to stop?

Perhaps you believe that your mind has to be brought to a complete stop in order for awakening to occur. Indeed, many believe that awakening means the mind has suspended its normal activity and only functions in a highly simplified manner focused on the task at hand. While that may be true for a certain type of awakening, it is not typically a feature of divinely human, embodied awakenings. We have discovered that, paradoxically, the mind can continue its thinking without interfering with a profound, tacit *knowing* of your infinite transcendent nature.

However, when the mind is hyperactive or compulsively running through thought-loops, it can be difficult or impossible to notice subtle experience or make the inquiries that will lead to clarifying your Conscious nature. This is when practices such as meditation, greenlighting, Inseeing, and psychotherapy that help release the bound energy that is driving the mind's activity are most useful. What then shifts is a certain amount of the background struggle or resistance to what is (which is experienced as mental pain or suffering) that is ongoing for most people most of the time. Calming the incessant yammering of the inner critic brings about a noticeable quieting of the mental noise most people assume is an inevitable part of life. Hallelujah!

Try this: using Inseeing to invite soul qualities

One of the most interesting potentials for Inseeing is that it can assist us in directly experiencing what we might call "soul qualities"—peace, love, spaciousness, joy, wellness of being, and many more. These states are natural and inherent in us, and known by our "body wisdom," though they may be obscured when our focus is caught up in our personal concerns and reactions.

Once you've had some practice with using Inseeing to bring warm, loving Presence to whatever issues or concerns are arising in you, you can begin using it to explore more unlimited states of Being. While your physical body is very much anchored in the physical realm, your subtle inner body is both Infinite and finite, a matrix of intelligent, aware energy that is continually registering the *whole* of every situation, including its inner meaning. Your body knows not only how to heal itself physically, but how to heal itself emotionally and spiritually as well—by integrating and opening those places that in the past were frozen in patterns of trauma and reactivity.

Beyond healing, your inner body also has access to all states of consciousness—they are part of its birthright, so to speak. Therefore you can use the same basic steps of Inseeing you learned in Chapter 5 to invite a felt sense of, for instance, wellness of Being. The key word here is "invite." Sometimes a shift into an expanded state will be possible and sometimes it won't. Please don't let that discourage you. Your body knows what is most important for you at any given time, and if you have pressing issues, they will usually need to be given attention before you will be able to invite a soul quality. Just try again at a later time.

To invite a soul quality, first you will want to come into a state of Presence and bring attention to your inner body (refer to Chapter 5 if you need a refresher on this step). If anything shows up strongly as "wanting attention right now," just explore that as usual. Your best opportunity for inviting an experience of a soul quality is when nothing is clamoring for attention. But if nothing is particularly intrusive—and this might happen at the beginning of a session or after you've spent some time with a part that needed attention—you might simply ask inwardly, "Would you show me wellness of Being right now?" (or wholeness, peace, love, joy, spaciousness, bliss, creativity, etc.), and be open to whatever comes. Just let yourself receive that.

You can take this one step further, and explore Presence itself. Of course, Presence, being that which is observing all the things and objects that arise into awareness, cannot itself be directly studied in the same way. Still, you have no doubt sensed the spaciousness, warmth, and interested curiosity that are qualities of Presence. Simply take some time to let yourself *be* those qualities. Relax your focus on what's arising, let go of noticing sensations, and let Presence turn in upon itself in deepest contemplation. You might discover that Presence is more than a state of consciousness, it is the deepest, truest aspect of Who You Are— that which is unchanging and always-ever-present, yet also intimately personal, warm, and caring. And this recognition is what forms the basis of divinely human awakening and embodiment.

Natural oscillations

It is the nature of glimpses to come and go. Once the wave of heightened awareness has faded, returning you to mundane "normal" consciousness, you may find yourself questioning whether anything about you is different at all. You may be dismayed to find that you still have an overly-active mind, or find yourself doubting the reality of your experience. You may, once again, feel adrift in a confusing world, or that you've lost access to that special dimension of awareness or that special sense of guidance from a loving archetypal being. It's easy to think that you've failed, yet again, to achieve your goal of a stable awakening.

But oscillations are a necessary part of the process. Because the vibrational frequency of a glimpse is (by definition) higher, or more refined, than your usual frequency, experiences at that level are seldom easily sustained or recreated at will. Your physiology needs to evolve also, developing greater capacity to sustain higher energy states without injury. Temporary shifts into heightened awareness "stretch" that capacity, so to speak, then recede for a while to allow for integration.

Besides that—and perhaps more importantly—when a special experience recedes, you are then required to search beneath the experiential nature of altered states in order to discover the Consciousness that is always ever present and unchanging—and coming fully awake in and as you. This is very important! *Embodied awakening isn't an experience or a state.* As long as you are holding out hope that you will somehow shift into a heightened state and stay there, you will be frustrated in your searching. States are always, by definition, temporary and changing, and embodied awakening is not an altered state but a permanent condition. Oscillations bring us the gift of taking away the shine and dropping us starkly back into our human condition.

Your work, during the "trough" times (as opposed to the peak times), is to discover Being as it expresses itself in all aspects of your life, the mundane and prosaic as well as the sublime. This may be difficult at first, but it is the very place that the lion's share of embodied awakening takes place. How do you do that? By giving as much attention to what you *know* as you do to how you currently *feel*. What is it that is always ever-present, no matter what's going on?

Interpreting spiritual experiences through your filters

A huge range of descriptions of spiritual experience can be found in the world's spiritual literature. When you are reading or listening to another's report, you might get confused and begin to doubt the validity of your own experience. However, there is a framework that may help you understand what is behind all of these differences so that you are not misled by them.

In the world of form, there's infinite variety. While there are universal themes and archetypes—good and evil, for instance— the specifics of how an archetype manifests vary among different cultures and different languages. Values change over time as well, and behaviors that one culture considers appropriate another culture may abhor. The different spiritual frameworks children are born into shape their worldview and color their experiences.

In contrast to all these variations and perhaps because of them, humans long to find something that is universally true, that transcends this plurality of values, something trustable no matter what. We desire to find an ultimate reality and then bring that level of understanding into our human interactions. This often drives our spiritual seeking and fascinates us with messiahs, or avatars: those who are ostensibly plugged into a universally-true level of understanding and able to share that truth with others.

We can posit that Consciousness is unmoving and unchanging, therefore universally and perpetually the source of "capital T" Truth (as opposed to more relative truths found in manifest reality). We can also assert that when someone has a profound revelation, they are partaking of a universal truth and having the same fundamental experience as any other person who opens to that level of spiritual experience. In other words, we can make a proposition that anyone who fully opens to Consciousness will know it in the same way as anyone else having that experience— because it is both universal and unchanging, hence always the same. But if that is so, why do there appear to be so many very *different* descriptions of spiritual experiences?

The answer lies not in the experience itself, which is formless, but in the way the mind interprets the experience afterward. Each person who has a mystical experience will interpret it through the spiritual tradition they grew up in or other archetypes that exist in our collective field, through their unique human psycho-emotional identity, and through their level of spiritual unfoldment.

When you have a direct apperception of Consciousness, the sense of being in the presence of that which is unshakably and universally *True* will most likely persist even as your mind is describing it in form and language that has meaning for you. When you understand this mechanism, you will be more able to look beneath the words of other realizers to the essence of what is being described. You can be inspired by what others are teaching without having to believe that it is the literal or ultimate truth (and yes, this applies to everything I'm writing in this book also!).

Bringing expectations down to earth

Another difficulty you may encounter on your quest for "enlightenment" may occur if you hold high expectations for how your life will feel. A peak experience stands above the ordinary ins and outs of daily life. As if suddenly soaring like an eagle above the landscape, the illuminated view is vast and untroubled by the sorts of concerns and details that generally interfere with inner peace. It's almost inevitable that spiritual seekers, once they've had a taste, hope to experience more of *that*. They often hang on to a fantasy—sometimes subconsciously—that one day they will be able to maintain that unbounded, blissful feeling as a permanent, unbroken state.

Some authors pen their accounts of "enlightenment" while still in the throes of an expanded state, glimpse, or other peak experience, as if it is a permanent state. If you could follow up with them weeks or months later, you might find they've landed back in their very human condition. If you only read their descriptions of sublime states, you might be led to expect your own awakening to come with a sustained feeling of bliss—and discount anything other than that.

Again, non-ordinary states are just that: out of the ordinary. They give us insights into the nature of reality and our relationship to it, but they are states, not permanent conditions. In the next chapter we will talk more about the permanent, irrevocable shift into non-separate conscious embodiment, and give a more grounded view of what is possible. While this may have the effect of downgrading your expectations, I do not mean to imply you must settle for something that does not fulfill your aspirations and potential. You will simply be better equipped to cooperate with the process if your framework is appropriate for the stage of development you are currently experiencing. All too many people have hoped for their transformation to come in one fell swoop at the hand of a divine agency that completely uproots all of their so-called "negative" tendencies without any effort on their part. As you observe the process of unfolding into being divinely human, you will find that, in most cases, it is more like a hero's journey through the trials of the underworld than it is about a sudden, wholesale elimination of the emotional highs and lows of human life.

What is Consciousness?

All great quests begin with something that is sought: the goal, the grail. The quest for enlightenment is no exception, and the goal might be "inner peace," "equanimity," "wisdom," "compassion," or "Consciousness" itself. Or "God." Whatever the particular quality that most draws a person, it will no doubt be something ineffable, although they might use terms that point to what it is NOT: not-bound, not-finite, not-limited. They are pointing to something outside of their ordinary separate, finite experience of being a human being, something they have either heard about or had a personal glimpse of, something they intuit would make a real difference in the quality of their life if they only could attain— or obtain—it.

Consciousness, however, is not and can never be an object to be sought, or a goal to be arrived at. This is because Consciousness does not exist at the same level of experience as all of the other things we can be aware of, even the ephemeral ones such as love, compassion, insight, and peace. Each of these has its own flavor, as it were, yet Consciousness stands beyond all flavors, all variation. Instead, Consciousness is the substrate upon which flavor, color, temperature, form, etc., all take shape. In addition, Consciousness is that which is aware of all the "things" that happen in our experience. None of this reality as we know it would be perceptible without the perceiver. Consciousness is the perceiver, and also that which makes perception possible.

This can be very tricky to articulate, and here again I ask your indulgence as I attempt to find words that might evoke something for you. Ultimately you will not be able to grasp this fully until your own revelatory experiences make it apparent. The human mind has very limited capacity to create a framework for something that is not an object. You will try and fail, and in failing, your mind will be inclined to use skepticism to throw the entire subject into doubt. However, you can begin with a willingness to abide with the not knowing, accepting that your logical thinking mind cannot know everything. And from that beginning, you can become a skilled observer of your own experience, without jumping to premature conclusions about what your experience means.

If we were to begin creating a concept-framework for Consciousness, we might describe it as the Prime Essence, that which is prior to or beneath even the tiniest particles that our quantum physicists are able to identify. It is a field of potential and potency, aware-ized energy, the very foundation of all life and all material in the universe. As such, it has no qualities whatsoever—because to give it any qualities would be to make it more limited, specific and finite than it is. In being without qualities, it cannot be seen, or felt, or experienced by human senses. It can only be intuited by a person who has cultivated their ability to sense into what lies beneath ordinary sense perceptions and day-to-day awareness.

Unmoving Absolute and dynamic Source/substance (two faces of God)

Having said that Consciousness is indescribable, as existing completely beyond anything humans can experience in the usual way, I'd now like to expand the framework a bit to include two "sides" of Consciousness. There is a still, unmoving side that is sometimes called the Absolute, and a more dynamic aspect that is sometimes called the Source—the essence energy of life and creation, or "Mother-Father-God-Goddess-All That Is."

A useful analogy is that the Ultimate is like a coin with two faces, different yet inseparably One. The still, unmoving Absolute can be likened to our own mind in which thoughts arise but which is itself without form or quality. Dynamic Source, on the other hand, can be experienced in the deepest mystical states as pure Light, pure vibrating Energy, or pure Love. To experience any of these qualities in their purest form usually requires cultivation, and is considered the *penultimate* experience (second highest). Then, if your experience goes deeper or *beyond* that, into the

Absolute, you will be unable to describe it in words, because there are no perceptible qualities to be reported or grasped by the mind.

Three primary aspects of dynamic Consciousness

As it begins to take form, Source-Consciousness refracts as if through a prism, giving rise to all the shapes and abilities that create the perceivable world. Of particular interest to those who are awakening is what I call the three primary aspects of Consciousness: Awareness, Being, and Heart. These aspects *do* have tangible qualities that are already to some degree experienced by all people.

Awareness has the qualities of clarity, intelligence, and **light** which enable anything to be experienced or known. Awareness is the means by which Consciousness continually registers everything which is arising as thoughts, feelings, and sensations in the field of perception, memory, or fantasy. It is without boundary, form, or content itself, and is sometimes characterized as an impersonal Witness. As it embodies, however, Awareness is experienced as a more personal sense of *Presence*, which is primarily sensed in the center of the head, although it permeates the area around the head as well.

Being provides our sense of existence in space-time, and its qualities include stillness, deep peace, and non-separateness. Being is vibrational life **energy**, the very sense of aliveness that is felt by all beings and is without boundary, form, or content. As the impersonal current of Being moves into embodiment, it becomes the *felt senses* that connect body with mind and allow for felt meanings to become apparent. While it can be felt anywhere in and around the body, the strongest experience of Being occurs in the belly, where what we call the "ground of Being" can most easily be felt.

Heart is the principle of unconditional **love**, and is often characterized as the divine Mother, the Goddess, or the Beloved whose welcoming embrace provides a much-needed balm for the soul. Heart is a multi-dimensional center that allows for everything from raw emotion, to subtle feelings, to the rarest, most exquisite divine frequencies. Heart's awakening may involve many steps to help it heal from the wounds it has sustained as a highly sensitive center of feeling. While Heart-essence is impersonal, infinite, and unbounded, as it embodies it is experienced most strongly in the center of the chest where it becomes very personal caring, tenderness, and *compassion* for the human predicament as well as our own personal suffering.

You will likely have easier access to, and awaken via, one or perhaps two of these aspects of Consciousness. The common thread through all of them is that their impersonal aspects are infinite and without boundaries—thereby making experience of non-separate Onlyness possible—while their more personal aspects are accessible here and now and are to some degree experienced by everyone. Awakening to any one of these aspects of Consciousness will give you access to the infinite, to the divine. While any of these are sufficient for embodied awakening, at some point you may be drawn to explore the other aspects as part of the natural unfoldment of your Conscious nature.

Inner divinity and the divine Other (I-Thou)

A natural outcome of an awakening experience could be an inclination to proclaim yourself to be God: I Am That. Which is true—in one sense. But don't forget that your human self can only know, interpret, and express a fairly limited range of what That is. What is more true is that you are of the *same essence* as That. That is the stuff of which you are made, and That is what is perceiving and experiencing as and through you, as well as being the essence of all that is perceived. We could make a case for saying ALL IS CONSCIOUSNESS, including you. And rightly enough. Yet for all practical purposes, there will remain an I-Thou relationship with the divine, because what any human can experience and demonstrate at any given time is but a fraction of the spirit/matter universe.

Glimpses are only the beginning

In other words, awakening will not turn you into God, nor will it merely enable you to realize your pre-existing oneness with the divine. It will bring your pre-existing divine nature into your full conscious awareness where it can become a living, creative force. In Chapter 10, I'll describe the fundamental shift of embodied awakening—from experiencing yourself as a separate, isolated human being to experiencing yourself as inseparable divinity coupled with finite humanity. While including the human parts of our experience may seem limiting, it also brings incredible richness to our experience. But it is not by choice that we do this anyway: it seems to be the very direction evolution is taking us.

10

DIVINELY HUMAN AWAKENING

Our Story: We took whatever actions were necessary and appropriate to grasp the means of our own Realization— the irrevocable whole-being integration of Infinite Conscious Presence with finite local matter (our humanness)—and became divinely human.

Consciousness awakens

There is a distinct, identifiable shift-point that occurs when your transpersonal Presence, which up till now has felt like a visitor that comes and goes, takes up permanent residence or "lands" in and as Who You Are. Your identity shifts from thinking yourself to be a separate human to a dual identity as both human and divine: simultaneously the conditioned self and the unconditioned, infinite, sublime essence that permeates all things and all beings. Over time, these two identities come to be experienced as "not two" and merge into an inseparable unity or Onlyness.

There is a difference between having an awakening experience (illumination) and having a permanent, irrevocable *embodied* awakening or "second birth." The latter is a non-reversible shift, whereas illuminating experiences are transient. Illuminations may bring life-changing new perspectives, but your divinely human, embodied awakening will completely shift the foundation from which you live.

Divinely human realization is based on a profound, experiential, whole-being recognition of your divine nature—that part of What You Are that is immaterial, infinite, unbounded, and without form or limitation. This is what brings the "divine" part of your divinely human self to full, lively awakeness, whereas prior to this realization it will have been as if sleeping. It was always there, but not an active part of your experience of yourself and your life on an ongoing basis.

Witnessing

"Witness" awakenings are frequently the result of meditation, or Advaitic-style inquiry into the question, "Who am I?" As you work your way through all the levels of who you have taken yourself to be in the past, you discover that none of the particulars about yourself is really adequate to convey the "you-ness" of you. There is an ineffable essence at the heart of who you are, and it isn't definable or objectifiable at all. As you contemplate the phenomenon of "you," you begin to realize that the patterns of your psycho-physical self are being observed by *something* or *someone* that stands somehow apart from them—at least sufficiently to be observing them. What is this? As the inquiry ripens, you may begin noticing that your very sense of *you*—the center that you live from—shifts over to this very ineffable essence that is witnessing your life as it unfolds. It is a real mystery, because everything you have studied up till this point has been something that you could look *at*, examine, and describe. Now you are sensing the very place from which the looking happens. Only it's not a place at all, of course. It's *nothing*. But it's a very rich nothing, a field full of potential that feels both totally familiar and totally new at the same time.

This "nothing" is your Conscious nature. It is also called Witness Consciousness or Awareness. (Some authors use the term Presence interchangeably with Awareness, though I use the term Presence more specifically, to refer to *embodied* Awareness—that which has the quality of being warm and caring.) Some people experience a vivid enlivenment of their Conscious nature as a result of transmission, inquiry, meditative cultivation, or even spontaneously out of the blue, when it is shining so brightly (so to speak) that it is unmistakable. Though this outshining may be a temporary phenomenon, it becomes a stable awakening when your sense of Self shifts out of its conditioned, historic way of experiencing your life to the free, unbounded essence-nature that is, instead, the *field* from which the conditioned self arises.

The awakening of Witness Consciousness is a significant accomplishment, but it alone does not complete the transformation into the divinely human condition. And what's more, it isn't required, as a separate, distinct experience, for embodied awakenings to happen. Useful, yes, but not required. Not everyone will have a distinct Witnessing experience, where the sense of identity distinctly shifts from their human personality to their essence nature. Some will awaken directly in the midst of their human experience.

Three avenues of embodied awakening

The term "embodied-feeling-witness-Consciousness," coined by senior Waking Down teacher Van Nguyen, is sometimes used to point to the manner in which your Conscious nature can come alive and awake right *in* your bodily experience. Though Consciousness has no manifest qualities in and of itself, people's experience of embodied Consciousness as it is awakening tends to be somewhat tangible via the *felt sense* of one of the three primary "flavors" that were described in Chapter 9. Remember, when Source-Consciousness approaches embodiment, it refracts as through a prism, creating Awareness (felt in the head), Being (felt in the belly), and Heart (felt in the area of the physical heart). Each of these aspects has the quality of being infinite, ever-existent, and without boundary, yet simultaneously can be experienced as energetic sensations within the body. Another way of saying this is that, from the relative human perspective, Consciousness is typically discovered through one of these three avenues of experience—whichever one becomes activated through spiritual cultivation.

The type of awakening, and the terms you use to describe it, will vary according to which of the three avenues you awaken through. This is useful information to keep in mind as you read other people's accounts of awakening: they may sound quite different from one another. But whether awakening Consciousness shows up as the light and clarity of Awareness, the subtle vibrational energy of Being, or the unconditional love of Heart, what is common to all these awakenings is that they remove the illusion of being separate or incomplete, and they open you to a dimension of your being that is infinite, unchanging, and without boundary.

Expectations can get in the way

One of the obstacles that can come up during this passage is an attachment to the more sublime or flashy experiences that you might have experienced along the way. If you think that awakening will land you permanently in a state of vastness, deep peace, sublime ecstasy, or other juicy quality, you might not recognize something less impressive as a real awakening. Or you might expect that awakening will leave you unbothered by the emotional turbulence of being human—the frustrations, the grief, the constant desiring, the volatile anger, the fears, etc. As long as this expectation is causing you to look "over there" for an awakening, you will tend to devalue or overlook what might very well be a true embodied awakening, right here, right now.

Mind cannot know, or figure this out

It may be useful at this point to simply accept that your mind will not be able to figure this out in advance—or even, possibly, for some time after. The way your awakening will synergize into conscious embodiment will surprise you. It may seem as if something new has come into your lived experience, and at the same time, it may feel pretty darn ordinary. As one student put it, "I've got to say, I'm under-whelmed." This is not to say it's less than an extraordinary shift. It *is* extraordinary! But generally it's not as flashy as our ever-desiring minds would like it to be, nor does it remove us from our humanness and the challenges of our day-to-day lives.

Paradox of simultaneity

So, if it's not about attaining a permanent state of detachment or bliss, what is it? One thing that changes upon embodied awakening is that, before a permanent shift, we seem to experience only one state at a time; either we're caught up in very familiar human thinking and emotional responses, or we're in an expanded state of bliss, peace, equanimity, infinitude, etc. There is an either-or quality. For the person on their way to becoming divinely human, these states tend to oscillate from one to the other. At times we're sure we're "it," and at other times we feel like we've "lost it."

A key element of embodied awakening is that we begin to live in the paradox of simultaneity. This means that our capacity somehow shifts, and we begin to know ourselves as infinite Being *at the same time* as we might, for instance, be experiencing irritation at being in the slow line at the supermarket. It's not really possible for the mind to imagine how this could be, until it can. One day you notice that no matter what you are experiencing, your sense of your divine self is never really gone. It might slip into the background of your awareness during periods of intense activity or emotional upset, but if you just stop and check inwardly, you recognize that it is still right there, humming along, confident in its own existence.

This quality of both/and—of being *both* infinite Consciousness *and* very individual human—is one of the hallmarks of the divinely human person. Instead of waking up into a Conscious nature that is somehow detached or silently witnessing from a remote location, unperturbed by all things physical, you find yourself awakening right *into* your human experience.

"Landing" in your divinely human condition

Sometimes embodied awakening comes with a vivid sense of "landing" or "flashing forward" right down into your heart and whole-being—belly, legs, toes, fingers, or simply all of your body. Some describe a sense of activation, or energy, in the area of the heart on the right side or near the center of the chest. There is a correlation between the physical location of the sino-atrial node of the heart—that special nerve plexus that is the origin of the signals that govern the heartbeat—and what some spiritual teachings hold to be the seat of the soul in the human body. It is also a place where many feel the tension of the core wound most acutely. Awakening correlates with the release or relaxation of this tension, and is often accompanied by a shift in the felt sense of the heart area in the body.

Some people describe a phenomenon where it feels as if their eyes are looking out from the middle of their chest, rather than their usual location in the head. However, it is not essential to have special effects for the awakening to take place. Each body is unique and will experience this shift of Conscious embodiment in its own way.

"Popping" vs. "oozing"

Sometimes a wholesale shift will occur in one fell swoop. Some have described it as if a bubble they had been encased in suddenly burst and the sense of being separate from everything else just vanished. Others have described a sudden shift from feeling like a person inside a universe to feeling like the Universe itself, with a person inside.

It is more common, and perhaps more trustable as a permanent awakening, for people to experience a series of smaller shifts and "aha's" over time, as the pieces of the awakening puzzle come alive for them. Perhaps they have an illumination that reveals the inherent Onlyness of everything: how still Witnessing and dancing manifestation are all made of one Conscious principle, and are inseparable from one another and all things. Or perhaps they feel their heart touched by divine love and compassion for all creation, and now realize that everything shares a fundamental unity. Perhaps they gradually come to realize that the Presence they have been using to explore their inner process is Who They Really Are—and everyone else is, too. Or perhaps they just gradually clear away the resistance they have been feeling, and discard the myths they've been hanging on to. When they take a fresh look, they realize the truth of what is— that they *are* divinely human and could not be otherwise.

Stories of awakening

I highly recommend a wonderful compilation of personal stories put together by Waking Down mentor Bob Valine, called *Dancing in the Fire: Stories of Awakening in the Heart of Community.* Find it on amazon.com, and then prepare to be amazed by the remarkable variety of awakenings that have occurred in "ordinary" people who are a lot like you and me.

The elements of non-separate conscious embodiment (a.k.a. the "second birth")

Because everybody is unique, and every body's experience of becoming Conscious will be unique, it can be difficult—in fact it is an art form—to help someone clarify when he or she has awakened into divinely human embodiment. There are many types of awakenings, and we don't mean to discount anyone's awakening experiences by calling them "not the second birth." However, it is also useful to make some discriminations, because focusing attention on all of the elements of a divinely human awakening can help to make it real and solid—a "realized" condition—rather than being a glimpse that is not yet a steady state.

The key elements that comprise the divinely human condition are 1) living in the paradox of simultaneity, 2) the end of seeking as you knew it, and 3) a recognition of the non-separate nature of Consciousness (Awareness, Being, or Heart) and phenomena. These aspects might arrive separately in random order, or they might happen all at once without the components standing out as distinct. But, however they happen, these three elements should be present and clear to you:

1. <u>Both/and.</u> I discussed the paradox of simultaneity earlier, and will not belabor it too much because either you will automatically resonate with that framework because it is true in your own experience, or you won't. Prior to this shift, you are only able to experience one state at a time, and after it, you become able to experience *both* your infinite divine Self *and* your finite, limited humanness at the same time. And by "experience" I don't mean simply "conceptualize"—it has to be your actual, lived experience.

2. <u>Seeking ends.</u> The end of seeking happens when you begin to trust that there *fundamentally* isn't anything more to "get" by seeking. I put it this way advisedly. Some people have a strong sense of having "found" what they were seeking, yet others may not have such a clear sense of that. However, everyone reports that their impulse to keep striving for a fundamental spiritual understanding has come to an end. Growth continues, but something very important and intrinsic to their sense of being whole has come alive in them and no longer has to be sought.

3. <u>Personal to transpersonal.</u> Initial experience of your Conscious nature may feel quite personal, as if *you* are having a peak experience, or an expansion of consciousness, that really doesn't have anything to do with anyone else or the world at large. Even the sense of living the paradox of simultaneity can seem quite personal and internal to you.

The transpersonal shift involves deeply contemplating the spacious, unlimited nature of Consciousness. Is it a personal experience only, or does that infinite quality occur without any demarcation points, such that what seems to be personal to you might be universally true for all beings and all of life? When the *universal* quality of Consciousness becomes real for you experientially, you will begin living fully as a divinely human being.

The challenge of conveying "simultaneity" using a linear language

Our linear language is an inadequate tool for conveying simultaneity, or the both/and experience that comes with embodied awakenings. For instance, it's difficult to speak my current thoughts and emotions while at the same time conveying my sense of being existentially free and trusting of Being. When I try, it takes a lot of words to do so. This is one of the reasons why people have been led to expect that awakening will be all about being free and transcending of their human dramas—because people experiencing the shift into an awakened condition often speak or write from the perspective of free Consciousness only. Unfortunately, if a spiritual teacher ONLY speaks from the perspective of Consciousness, they do not give much help to our ongoing struggle to integrate human thoughts and emotions with the radical shift into a new mode of being.

Other types of awakenings

Not every awakening is oriented to embodiment. Becoming divinely human is NOT everyone's goal or result. It appears that there may be a choice point where you can move toward mutuality and embrace humanness, or dissociate from that humanness in order to live predominantly in transcendence. As in a cave in the Himalayas. That type of awakening may require continual vigilance lest the thinking, reacting mind comes in to disturb the inner equilibrium. Because the conditioned tendencies of being human are quite entrenched for most people, it seems that few people are able to become truly established in transcendental awakening for very long. Besides, when you are hanging out in the transcendent, who is supposed to be living your life?

The core wound is the gateway to embodied awakening

The path to embodied awakening is through the core wound, which was introduced in Chapter 3.

You may remember that the core wound is the result of our existential condition of being both infinite Consciousness and finite human being. When unconscious, the core wound is that feeling of distress at the core of your being, that subtle driver of human endeavor and escapism, that "ugh" that we REALLY don't want to feel. You must consciously enter the core wound, in order to enter the kingdom of the divinely human life. Sure, experiencing the freedom and bliss of your Conscious nature can be an important step along the way, one that will give you a much bigger sense of the totality of Who You Are. But we are talking here about nothing less than birthing that infinite Consciousness into your very finite human body to inaugurate a whole new way of being and acting in the world. Instead of your small self reaching upward to contact the big Self, you are now inviting that big Self to come home and inhabit your body in a much more direct and empowered way than ever before.

That *embodying* will necessarily include inhabiting the core wound. And as long as your sense of self—your human, personal self—is averse to feeling the core wound, and is actively avoiding it, it will not be possible for your Bigger Self to fully land here. (Work with me here on the language, okay?) That's why a big part of the work of divinely human awakening is facing your shadow parts and welcoming them home, thereby releasing bound energy and increasing your capacity to be with all of your feelings—the uncomfortable ones as well as the pleasant ones. As you go deeper with your inquiries, you get down to the impersonal aspects of the core wound itself, the feelings of "not-good-enoughness," or incompleteness, that have kept you from being able to fully own the wonder that you are. You have to fully drop into these difficult places. You have to let yourself realize that the discomfort of being Infinite within the boundaries of a vulnerable human body is not due to your personal failings, but is inherent in being human, and more or less ever-present and inescapable. You have to face all the ways you have tried to jump out of these feelings, and truly give up that effort, in order to prepare a home for Being to abide in and as *you*.

A final note: even though you may understand that you must encounter the core wound in order to experience a new birth, you cannot do it as a technique to get out of your human predicament. Then it would be just another strategy for avoiding the real impact of that very predicament—to avoid really *being here*. And as long as you're avoiding being here, you will be working against the impulse of Being to come awake here. You are working against your awakening. But hey, that's only natural, given that you ARE a human being and can hardly avoid your intrinsic tendency to want to avoid discomfort.

So you will avoid the core wound as long as you are able to. That seems to be how it goes. But at some point, you will run out of the ability to keep doing that, and become more interested, and more able, to face the predicament of your human condition. As you realize that it is okay to feel the core wound, you surrender all of your struggle, your fight, and your impulse to escape. You find yourself accepting that you are the limited one you are, that it's not your fault, that it's really okay, and that you're *lovable exactly as that*.

And it's not so bad after all.

Try this: Inseeing into your core wound

Take a moment to bring your attention to your body. Perhaps sense the feeling of your feet contacting the floor, and the feeling of your clothing against your skin. With a nice full breath, feel your chest expanding and the sense of enlivenment that comes.

Next, take some time to register the complex feeling of all of you—all of your life right now. You may feel any variety of body sensations, and thoughts or images may flash through your mind. If you become aware of any issue, say an inner hello to it and see if it would be okay with you coming back to it later. The core wound isn't about issues, even deep-seated ones.

Take a moment to think of the good things in your life, be they material things, the work that you do, or people or pets that you love. Notice how you want to hold onto those things, even though you know they will not be with you forever.

Now think of things in your life that you'd like to be free of— those things that are irritating or painful, or the ways you feel stuck. Include feelings of insufficiency, incompleteness, or "not-good-enoughness." Notice how difficult it is to live with these things.

Invite any fears that you might have about scary events in the future: loss of income, ill health, or the loss of loved ones. And include any feelings of being separate, either from Source or from other people, and how cut off and isolated that can make you feel.

Now consider all of these things as a whole. Can you see how all of these elements together create a continual stress or tension at the core of your being? Continue to bring your attention inward, ever more deeply. As if, out of all the sensations you are mindful of, you could distill out the core feeling of being you.

And now take a moment to remember Presence. You are *also* that which can be mindful of all these things, that which can bring interested curiosity and deep caring to anything and everything that arises in you throughout the course of your life. You are the tension and also the field in which the tension is occurring. And the tension of the core wound does not need to be resolved.

"Grasping the means of your own awakening"

Because your body is unique, and comes to this point of ripeness for awakening through its own novel path and history, you will need to find your own individual route to and through this transformative passage.

When Saniel left the fold of his former teacher, Adi Da, he began looking for guidance from some other source. He was quite fortunate in finding a wise mentor who advised him, "Saniel, you have to grasp the means of your own realization!" And by that, he opened Saniel's eyes to the possibility of not relying on any other authority above his own instincts and intuitive sense to lead him to exactly the right opportunities and support for completing his realization.

This doesn't mean that you should steer away from people who offer you support and advice, but that you should stay in touch with your own inner knowing and sense of rightness, and let that be your ultimate guide. You may be drawn to explore any number of different avenues of inspiration for your awakening process, some of which we described in Chapter 9.

You may want to experiment with letting go of any formulaic practices you have been relying on, at least for a while, to see what comes up if you aren't using them. Again, this doesn't mean those practices are not useful—they may have great value for you, and you may wish to either continue them or pick them up again after a period of experimentation without them. But any spiritual practice that you have been doing by rote, that hasn't brought awakening, might be working at cross purposes in some fashion, and it can be worthwhile to see what comes up when you just let yourself *be*, exactly as you are, for a while.

The most important point here is that when you are becoming divinely human, what matters most is who you are and what is arising in you, in this moment, that needs to be addressed in order to help free up your energy and attention to complete your awakening.

Clearing away final resistances to awakening

There may come a time when the various elements of this transformation appear to be in place—experientially known by you—but there is no discernable quantitative shift. Perhaps some places of resistance need to be addressed before your human self will feel safe enough to permit this shift. You may find yourself wondering about some of the following issues. If any of them resonate, why not bring them into your next Inseeing session to find out what they're trying to accomplish or wanting you to know?

• *Will I find myself alone?* This is a natural, instinctive fear that if you change, you will be unable to relate to your family and friends as you have in the past—or that they will be unable to see and relate to the new you. There is some basis for this fear, because relationships that were built on your conditioned personality relating to their conditioned personalities may indeed change as you become more able to live from your natural essence and less willing to keep living out of old patterns that are no longer relevant to the newly-emerging Self. The bad news is that some relationships may end, but the good news is that those relationships that end were ones where you were not seen and appreciated for being who you really are. And whenever something moves out of your life, space opens for something new to enter. Those who are drawn to the awakening you will be people who DO value who you now are.

• *Will I have to become someone else?* The patterned, conditioned aspects of your personality may be afraid they will be replaced by some mysterious Other that might not do as good a job of keeping you safe (which has been their job until now). It may take some time for them to come to trust that the Self that is awakening is the deepest aspect of who you are, and who you have always been. Rather than feeling like a personality transplant, the new quality of Being generally feels like what's most truly "you"— yet was previously held under wraps or in the background. The birthing of this essential nature doesn't automatically do away with patterns that function to promote survival—and this simple recognition may give enough reassurance to the vulnerable self for this shift to occur.

• *Will I have to step up to some special destiny?* Your awakening may come with a sense of destiny, as if you are stepping up to a new level of being and contributing in life. This might feel enlivening, or it might seem scary, as if there is some grand purpose lurking on the other side of awakening, a purpose you might not want or feel ready to undertake. Simply being willing to BE HERE fully, in a world that does not generally see or value such awakenings, is a heroic act in and of itself. You may be intuitively sensing the cosmic importance of such an act, and feeling it as a sense of destiny. And you may indeed have a calling to make a bigger contribution than you have in the past. What's important to know is that you won't be required to do anything you are not ready or willing to undertake. Most likely, if there is something new coming into your life that is part of your destiny, it will feel tailor-made to who you are and what you most value. You will feel excited to take it on, and the qualities you need to fulfill it will show up in a synchronistic way.

• *I'm not ready, adequate, or good enough.* Many people will encounter self-doubt as they find themselves changing and opening to what feels like nothing less than their own divine nature. And given that many of us have been told throughout our lives that we have to be "good" to earn spiritual rewards, it's no wonder that we would harbor some deep-seated doubts about whether we're good enough for this shift. Fortunately, embodied awakening is not something you have to earn through merit. You are already everything you need to be, and it is enough.

• *Who am I to think I'm worthy of this?* The flip side of self-doubt is a concern about being arrogant, which is taboo in many religions. "If I say I deserve this awakening, I am being arrogant and that's not allowed; people will find out that I'm nothing special and put me down" (or some variation on that theme). The truth is that if you find yourself in the midst of this transformation, Being has determined that it's your time. It has nothing to do with thinking you are worthy, or with what anyone else might think. It is taking place at a deeper level than that, a whole-being level that has little or nothing to do with what your mind thinks about it.

• *If I claim to be awakened, something bad might happen to me.* There is a primordial fear in our collective psyche that may turn up as you approach your awakening. In the past, people who dared to reveal their special qualities of insight or intuition, or their sense of being a divine person, were sometimes feared, persecuted, or killed. Perhaps foremost in our Western cultural history is the story of Jesus, who was crucified for proclaiming himself to be the son of God. It is good to bring fears of this type into full awareness, where they can be held up to the reality of our current situation. At least in the West, we have unprecedented freedom of belief, practice, and speech right now, which is a great blessing and opportunity.

• *I think I still have to do _____ (fill in the blank) before I can awaken.* This is especially likely to crop up if you have been oriented to doing extensive spiritual practices to refine and purify yourself in order to attain special states of consciousness. You may not think you have done enough yet for an awakening. Perhaps in the past extensive purification work was necessary. However, what we have been discovering, and have many examples of, is that extensive purification is seldom necessary, and this awakening is just bursting out all over the place in the most un-purified people. This is not meant to minimize anyone's attainment, but to emphasize that a highly refined degree of self-improvement does not appear to be required for this awakening.

• *This can't be it—it's too easy (and too ordinary).* This concern can be a real block to recognizing a divinely human awakening, especially in its early stages before it has been established, deepened, and integrated into a settled self-knowing and confidence in Being. Most seekers have created an expectation of something quite extraordinary, because much of what's written about "enlightenment" is speaking about a) peak experiences, b) transcendent conditions that have particular qualities of bliss, peace, disinterested witnessing, etc., or c) awakenings that have matured into a fully-developed condition. Remember, becoming divinely human will not be like anything you imagined, so what is most helpful is to stay attuned to what IS true in your experience, without comparing it to what others have described, or whatever your own expectations might have been.

• *If I validate this awakening as it is, I will be settling for something less than I want.* It is very important to make a distinction here, that the second birth is just that—a birth. Yes, it is a deep reckoning with what is, and it is a profound realization of your divinely human condition that encompasses both an exquisite infinity of awareness or aliveness and a very sobered appraisal of your human limitations. Yet in its early stages, it may feel pretty ordinary, as if you haven't changed at all but merely have a different perspective on what was always the case. But you HAVE shifted into a new capacity of experience and perception, and it will continue to evolve and refine itself over time, as you integrate all the elements that make up who you are now. This awakening is not an end point, but rather an *entry* point that will reveal many more dimensions as you continue to evolve over time.

• *My process isn't as _____ (dramatic, flashy, juicy, special, etc.) as so-and-so's, so it must not be an awakening.* It's easy to get caught up in comparing your process with what's happening in someone else's process, and to feel dissatisfied with your own. Remember that every body is different, and every awakening process is unique, so bring your attention back to your own experience, which is all that really matters for you.

Your landing platform

I spoke earlier of this awakening as a landing, as if your essence-self lands in your body and begins living here, as you.

Well, much like a helicopter needs a flat, solid surface on which to land, your awakening/landing will be facilitated by having good support structures in place in your life. While there's no hard-and-fast rule, it seems that Being tends to hold itself back a bit when your life is unstable or in times of major transition. Ideally, you will have an established home space that feels good to you, a job that's not too stressful or other source of income to meet your needs, the support of family and friends who understand what you are undertaking, and enough health and free time to devote to inquiry and mutual explorations with others of like mind.

It's not necessary to have everything just so, however. Being is resourceful, and can make do with a wide range of situations. However, if your awakening seems to be stalling, this is an area to look at. Perhaps some changes will be in order to create just the right kind of platform for *your* awakening process to unfold in an optimum way.

Divine timing

Remember, no matter how far you've come in your understanding, no matter how many illuminations you have experienced and resistances you have cleared, the timing of awakening is always by grace alone. No one can control it or predict it with accuracy.

Some people just seem to pop into awakening fairly quickly, with seemingly little effort, while others spend years and get utterly frustrated at how awakening seems to elude them, despite their best efforts. It's easy to feel jealous when others around you awaken more quickly! What gives?

The timing of awakening is a mystery, pure and simple. Perhaps it is a karmic thing, or perhaps it's related to particularly difficult conditioned patterns that persist in getting in the way. Whatever the reason, it is unlikely that it has much, if anything, to do with whether you are a "good practitioner."

Keep in mind that awakening is an ongoing process, and that you are "becoming divinely human" all along the way. For everyone who awakens, there will be a gradual process over time of bringing greater light, and greater depth of awareness, into the life they are living.

Oscillations

As mentioned in Chapter 9, a natural part of the awakening process is that times of illumination, or times when Being flashes forward into obvious embodiment, are typically followed by periods that feel most ordinary, as if you had "lost" whatever awakening you had experienced.

If you are beginning to think that you already have most of the elements of an embodied awakening in place, but are concerned that you still "lose it" from time to time, it may be a good opportunity to do a little research. In the early days following the shift, it is still easy for reactive patterns to get triggered and temporarily obscure the felt sense of the awakened condition. In other words, what is in the foreground of your awareness when you are calm and un-triggered naturally recedes into the background when there is some emotional or mental storm going on. This does *not* necessarily mean that you've lost your awakening.

You might check it out. As the storm abates, sense backward. Might there still have been an inner knowing of your divinely human nature, even during that period? If you could have hit the pause button on your reactivity, would your awakeness still have been present? Do you have a sense that it never was really gone? If the answer is yes, it might be time to consider whether you've experienced the second birth: the permanent, irrevocable shift of divinely human awakening.

Second birth conversations

There is a tradition in the Waking Down in Mutuality community of inviting people to have their awakenings vetted by a Waking Down teacher. Several teachers have developed particular skill in the art of helping someone determine whether a permanent second birth has occurred, and are available for clarifying conversations. You can find them at **wakingdown.org/contacts.**

Evaluating second births can, understandably, be a controversial practice. On the one hand, awakening is, practically by definition, self-validating. If you aren't convinced, what's the point? If Being is really awake in and as you, it will very likely be proclaiming itself internally: "I'm here! I'm here!"

But humans are complex, and even when awakening is shining forth, there may well be other parts of you that haven't yet got the message, that may still be doubting or resisting what is occurring. In that case, it can be most useful to have someone to talk with about the changes you are experiencing, and where you can explore the various aspects of awakening with someone who can help you discover what is really true for you. It's not about passing or failing, or getting some kind of stamp of approval. Your awakening is your own experience, and the idea is to help you gain clarity about the process, for your own benefit.

Many people report that the second birth conversation is a powerful rite of passage for them. In the act of finding words to describe the changes they've been undergoing, and then claiming what's happened as true for them, there is often a further deepening of the awakening itself. Speaking it makes it more REAL.

Another benefit of clarifying your second birth is that the focus of your inner dynamic will be shifting from seeking to integrating. Resolving any confusion can free you to take the next steps that are most appropriate for you now.

Of course, no one is required to get this kind of external validation of what is, essentially, a very private, personal experience. Confirmation of your second birth is only required if you are interested in taking the special courses offered by the Institute of Awakened Mutuality for people in the second life or if you are considering becoming a Waking Down mentor or teacher. But whether required or not, you may well want to take advantage of the opportunity, for the many benefits it will bring.

Confidence in Being

Although it's an important milestone, Saniel called this divinely human awakening "the second birth" for a reason. In many ways, it's just a birth into a new capacity and framework of living—a birth that is going to require a lot of growing before it becomes full-grown and fully-expressed. It is important to remember that this awakening will NOT immediately transform you into someone with all the answers and who is free of all conditioning and ego. Sorry! There is still work to do. It's an awakening because our essence does, indeed, awaken and become an active player in our daily lives. But keep in mind that this is "only" an initiation into a new stage of life, a beginning that will take much loving attention before it comes into its full fruition. No doubt at some point your "where's the enlightenment?" button will be pushed—and that's because divinely human awakening is a beginning, not an end point.

Confidence and trust in Being increases over time, eventually becoming unshakably stable, permeating and informing all of life. How that happens is the topic of our next chapter.

11

INTEGRATION

Our Story: We endured some challenging passages of integration, as our newly-awakened divine nature began reconfiguring our whole being so that we could embody greater freedom, wholeness, compassion, and love.

Integrating your divinely human awakening

The shift into the divinely human orientation is only a beginning. It must be integrated before the potential it offers can begin to be fully expressed.

Prior to the shift, you were primarily operating out of two energetic bodies (matrixes): gross (physical/ emotional), and subtle (mental/psychic). Regardless of which modality was dominant, those were the main frameworks of your experience. With this shift into divinely human awakening, a third, causal (spiritual/formless) energy body comes fully on line, and it brings with it a new set of potentials, sensitivities, and perceptual abilities. At this point, your operating system needs some time to work out the kinks so that all three energy bodies can function optimally in light of the new parameters.

Among the new qualities that will become more available over time is a greater sense of direct knowing, or insight, that doesn't depend on logic or emotional responses to discern the truth. It is an inner felt sense of "rightness" or "wrongness" that isn't about judging in a moral sense, but about discerning what is true for you personally. It's not about beliefs. This is a deep sense of what's true in the marrow of your bones, what matters, what's right for you. And perhaps what's right for the world, as well.

It's unlikely that this change will show up immediately in a full-blown form; instead, it will gradually develop over time. You will encounter this new configuration as you are trying to figure out how to live your awakening, and it may be puzzling at first. You may not get any direct sense of "what to do," but it is likely that you will begin to know, beyond any doubt, what is not right for you. The inner no's are often stronger at first than the yes's.

The good news is that you don't have to know how to make integration happen—your whole being will naturally bring you what you need for your most auspicious unfoldment. Much like puberty, your body-mind knows on some level how to navigate these changes. Patience and understanding will be your most powerful allies during this challenging time.

Another way of saying this is that Consciousness claims and inhabits the body-mind in a way it never has before. It's more intimate and more immediate, more up-close-and-personal. I'm not saying that you will be taken over by some alien agency. By now you hopefully realize that your Conscious Self is the self that has always felt the most true to you, the most core-level *you*. By awakening this deep Self, you're helping it come forward into manifestation so that it is able to live and breathe and act in the world, where in the past it might only have whispered its words of inspiration to you in the most subtle ways.

However, awakening in and of itself does not magically transform patterns of thinking and behavior established over a lifetime. That is the job of the integration period. While "how you've shown up" has been adequate to your life up till now (whether you have felt satisfied in your life or not, you've been *sufficient* or you wouldn't still be here), there are likely areas of wounding and survival patterning that no longer feel authentic. As you begin to move and express your greater wholeness, you will bump up against these tight places or knots in your psyche, and feel the impulse to find greater ease and freedom.

Honeymoon period

At the time of awakening, you may experience a grace period, or "honeymoon," that lasts days or months (and for a rare few, years), when the feeling-quality that arises from the intersection of your Conscious divine self and your physical body-mind is primarily ease and wellness of being. You may experience a release of lifelong tension or fear at a deep core level, and marvel at the freedom you feel. This wonderful phase is often described in spiritual literature as the pearl of great price, the gift of enlightenment.

However, the human side of the divinely human equation will reassert itself at some point, sooner or later, because its patterns run very deep in the psyche. There are some similarities with falling in love. For a brief glorious period, we are euphoric and see ourselves as our lovers see us—wonderful and magical, with all of our goals and aspirations within our grasp. But as always happens, "reality" resurfaces along with its inherent self-doubt, distrust, and other painful limits.

Where did the sense of freedom and ease go? At this point, it is only natural to fear that you have "lost" your awakening. And maybe to conclude that this realization isn't all you were expecting.

"Lemon of a realization"

Saniel tells the story of a woman who, in the early days of his teaching work, had her "second birth" only to fall smack dab into the pain of her brokenness. One day she brought a bowl of lemons to one of Saniel's sittings. As she set the bowl before him, she said, "Thanks, Saniel, for giving me a lemon of a realization!"

No matter how many times you're cautioned that embodied awakening isn't going to suddenly remove all of your conditioning and broken zones, nor put you into a permanent state of bliss, you may continue hoping that it will do just that. And when that doesn't happen, you may feel a keen sense of disappointment or disillusionment.

Feeling this way after experiencing the unconditional positivity that often temporarily accompanies embodied awakening is totally understandable. We naturally crave the experiences of openness, relaxation, trust, compassion, hopefulness, and intimacy that are possible when we are not being run by the conditioned states of contraction, anxiety, distrust, fear, and animosity which we might have been more familiar with in our life to date. It's normal to want to abide permanently in the more "positive" states, but it just isn't possible—no matter how much you might wish it to be so.

Is it permanent?

If your awakening was a true shift into the divinely human condition, you will never lose it because it is a stage shift, not a state. States come and go, whereas stages are progressive and only evolve in the direction of greater complexity and coherence. However, as mentioned in the previous chapter, it is common to experience oscillations as you are nearing the shift point. It is possible that an outshining of Consciousness could be mistaken for an awakening shift, in which case it could subside again, leaving you back in "ordinary human consciousness." This will not be a problem for long, because chances are you *will* naturally stabilize or hit the point-of-no-return sometime soon.

Occasionally, an awakening that is in progress will fail to fully bloom. Perhaps a life crisis intervenes and requires all of your attention and energy, so your spiritual progress gets tabled for a while (though some crises seem to catalyze deeper awakenings, so there is no rule of thumb here). Or perhaps for one reason or another you pull back from the experience, isolate yourself, and occupy your time so as to minimize exposure to the tectonic forces attempting to forge your divinely human Beingness. We see this sometimes in people who avoid mutuality, or who avoid claiming their awakening. At least in theory, you can sideline your awakening for some prolonged period. However, if you are destined to awaken, you are unlikely to be able to delay it indefinitely, and will probably find yourself increasingly uncomfortable until you lean into the potential that is available to you.

Feeling like you "lost it"

So, to recap, you cannot undo an embodied awakening once it has occurred, though at times it may FEEL as if you have lost it because of the arising of unwelcome states that you had hoped were gone for good. It can be very puzzling to feel fear, for instance, once you've discovered your essential invincibility as Being. Or to feel distrust of others once you've recognized fundamental non-separateness. Or to feel the pain of lack in the light of infinite abundance, or the sting of self-doubt or shame when you've discovered your fundamental goodness and divine right to be here exactly as you are.

What happens is that the momentum inherent in these conditioned states is causing them to reappear in your experience, generally when some aspect of your life triggers them into activity. Remember, this is one of the main ways by which you are programmed to survive as a biological entity. Humans are pattern-formers and pattern recognizers: whenever a situation appears on our radar, we subconsciously scan to see if it is similar to a past situation that was dangerous or in which we experienced injury. If so, the past situation gets overlaid upon the present one, bringing with it the full complement of distressed feelings that occurred during the original event.

I discussed these "broken zone" experiences in Chapter 5. What's new after the shift is that the embodiment of Presence provides an ever-greater capacity to re-experience these broken places of the psyche. You may think you've completed your healing work with a particular issue only to find it showing up again, even more stark, raw, and intense than before. Although you might feel discouraged by this turn of events, it is actually a wonderful opportunity. It turns out that the only time an old trauma can be fully released and healed is when it is fully activated—when you are re-experiencing it vividly. There seems to be an intelligence of Being that brings these opportunities forward as part of fully landing in, and integrating, your awakening.

Deeper passages

In order to have an embodied awakening, you will have faced and surrendered your resistance to feeling the core wound. However, there will likely be other deep-seated issues that you are still resisting, or trying to deny or override with cheery positive counter-thoughts. Being will find a way to bring you an encounter with them—not out of perversity, but out of its natural reach toward freedom and wholeness. Saniel calls this integration phase the "wakedown shakedown" because some of these passages can be quite challenging. Deep-seated issues can take weeks or months to fully surface from the depths where they have been hiding.

Ultimately, given time and perseverance (and skillful support) you will have met and mapped the territory of your shadow pretty well, and gained a degree of release from many of your traumas. And the light of Presence in you, as you, will continue to grow ever stronger. Think of a dimmer switch on a lamp. Awakening turns the light (of Presence) on to its lowest setting, and while it never goes out, strong obsessive thoughts or emotional storms can obscure the light. However, as you progress through the integration phase, the light gets gradually dialed up until emotional storms are no longer able to obscure it. At this point, you will no longer question whether you might have lost your awakening, because you will know Presence is always there, always available, always underlying, registering, and supporting all of your experiences. The strength of your now-awakened Presence will both draw more things to the surface for healing, and give you a greater capacity to be with whatever shows up.

Exquisite sensitivity

You may find yourself to be more aware and sensitive now, as if the buffers you used to have in place—those ways you were protected from feeling things too strongly—have been removed and now your skin is thinner and more permeable, and your encounters more stark and immediate than ever before. This sensitivity is part of coming fully alive and awake; sort of like waking up a foot that had gone to sleep. You certainly notice it!

Your emotions may be more raw and close to the surface, as well. Perhaps you cry more easily, for instance, or flare into anger more often than you used to. Or you are really moved by a story, or a piece of music, or a poem—being easily transported into that other reality, with full-heart and full-feeling. And your empathy for the plight of others might be especially strong these days.

Although you might feel like you're coming undone at times, successfully navigating the upheavals and storms of this integration phase is possible, and will be aided by continuing what you've been doing with greenlighting, Inseeing, and bringing compassionate Presence to whatever is arising.

Primal insanity

Your shakedown may go so deep that, at some point, you begin to fear that you are losing your grip on reality. You get inside your own dysfunctional patterning to such an extent that you start experiencing what you might call "craziness." This can be a frightening recognition, but it doesn't mean that you are uniquely handicapped—we ALL have some degree of insanity lying, usually, beneath the threshold of awareness. Encountering it in a vivid way can be very unsettling, and this is when it will be most important to have a good support team. Your support system may, for a while, have to supply perspective and good judgment when your own inner navigation system is proving unreliable. In other words, *it is important to have a support system that is stronger than the voice of your primal insanity.*

When you meet and integrate these "crazy" parts of yourself, you will become very strong, knowing that you are inherently intact even if there are parts of yourself that don't know that. Please use this information only as cautionary, not as predictive or as something to scare you away from embodiment. Yes, this process can get intense at times. After all, it IS a hero's journey, and at times it will feel daunting to dive deeply into your own underworld. But you can and will survive, and far more than that. You will blossom into a whole, intact, deeply-feeling person who can, in turn, help support others through their own hero's journey.

It's a good idea, before things get particularly difficult, to find a skilled and trusted therapist to guide you, so that your passage is no more difficult than it needs to be.

Divinely YOU emerging

With awakening, your old conditioned personality gets dismantled, bit by bit. As the reconfiguration goes ever deeper, you become freer to be more creative, more expressive, and more authentic than ever before. You may experience some confusion for a while, however. After all, who are you if not who you've always been?

You may discover the answer to that question not as an idea but by observing how you begin to show up in the situations you find yourself in. You may be surprised by what tumbles out of your mouth, for instance, or find yourself signing up to do something you never would have considered doing in the past. Or maybe new boundaries show up, and it becomes easier to say "no" to things that would previously have drained your energy. Take some time to get to know yourself in this new incarnation of you. I bet you'll be pleased with each step you take that expresses what feels real and authentic.

New encounters

It's important to give the newly-emerging YOU support at this time. Find out what nurtures you—what recharges your batteries, relieves your tension, and makes your body say "Yum!" It is every bit as important to your long-term wellness to include pleasure and play as it is to face the scary parts of your deep psyche. Perhaps even more so, because it will help counterbalance the inevitable stress of being fully here as a physical being in a challenging environment.

You may find yourself drawn to explore new situations and/or new relationships at this time. New interests may show up, or old interests that you had set aside and practically forgotten once again call to you. People who have known you for a long time typically expect you to behave in familiar ways, but when you are with new people, there can be more freedom to be, and freedom to experiment and play with who you are becoming.

Sometimes the impulse to explore new possibilities will carry you toward a new intimate relationship in which you are (hopefully) fully seen and met as a whole and divinely human person. A powerful tantric relationship can, indeed, help bring you forward into embodiment in profound ways. (See Chapter 7 for more about tantric initiations.)

However, if you are in a committed relationship and find yourself being attracted to someone new, please do not assume that it means you have to ditch your current relationship for a new one. Sometimes a tantric flare-up is just a symbol, a message from the part of you that longs to be fully seen and met, or to be more freely expressed in relationship. Many have turned that same passion and fire back into their current relationship, discovering more potential for real engagement there than they had thought possible.

Try this: inner yes's and no's

To help you discover what's most alive for you now, you might take some time to start noticing your inner yes's and no's. A good time to practice this is when you have a choice to make between two options that are not too weighty. For example, trying to decide whether to go see a movie or go out to dinner.

Begin with a pause. Perhaps take a nice full breath as you close your eyes and begin to sense inwardly. Take a minute to let your attention go to your feet, then your hands, then to the sense of contact between your hips and your chair. However that works best for you. Then bring your attention inward, into the area that includes your throat, chest, stomach, and belly.

With your attention resting in this area, notice the vague, undefined sense of the whole of your life right now. And then bring in the first option, going out to a movie. Imagine the experience: arriving at the theater, buying your ticket, the aroma of hot popcorn, the carpeted hallway, the darkened theater, the anticipation, and then the sensory wash of the movie's sights, sounds, and storyline. And now notice the overall feel of your inner body. Is it more *full*—as in full of energy or light—or more *flat*—as in tired or deflated?

Then switch and do the same thing with the other option. Imagine the experience of going out to eat: arriving at the restaurant, being seated by the waitperson, scanning the menu, interacting with a friend, ordering, anticipating and then eating a delicious meal. And notice the feeling of your inner body. Is it more *full* or more *flat*?

No matter what you normally prefer, your body's response will be unique in any given moment. With practice, you will get to know your own body's way of saying yes and no.

Of course, there will be times when following the yes wouldn't be advisable. Given a choice between a day at the beach and a day at the office, your body might prefer to play hooky. In a case like that, you might acknowledge what your body wants even while choosing to honor your work commitments. But when it's practical, you might try going with your inner body's yes's and avoiding the no's, and see what happens in your life. By tuning into your yes's and no's, you are inviting a fresh, whole-being perspective instead of relying primarily on your mind's habitual leanings. Let your body show you what it likes, and, in turn, embodiment will come more alive for you.

Governing sentimentalities

During the darkness before dawn, you began encountering some pretty tough limits, the places where you couldn't just intend a change and make it happen. You were being unraveled at the core, and surrender became the name of the game for a while, rather than empowerment.

Once you have awakened, this process of coming up against your most deeply broken places continues. You might even find yourself in the midst of a deep, prolonged passage where you can't really see an end in sight. This is a time of encountering your *governing sentimentalities,* the unconscious assumptions you've held about life that have been coloring everything—the ones you really didn't want to acknowledge, but down deep really believed.

*Example: About 9 months after the shift into conscious embodiment, Michael found himself plunged into a deep, black time that felt a lot like depression. He lost his ability to take pleasure in much of anything, or to motivate himself to do anything constructive. He felt flat, and his life felt meaningless and empty. He was aware that most of his life up to that point had been a search for meaning and joy—in other words, something in him had been trying to **disprove** his belief that life was meaningless. His quest for awakening was itself an attempt to bring fundamental meaning and purpose to his life.*

However, once he had fulfilled his seeking impulse, he found himself confronted with the even deeper dilemma— that his life still felt empty and meaningless. He could no longer hope that awakening would make it better. He was confronted with the stark "reality" of life's fundamental meaninglessness, and his own aversion to that fact. His depression was compounded by assuming other people had more joy and sense of purpose than he did, and that he was somehow seriously flawed.

Gradually, he discovered that "meaningless" wasn't automatically bad. "Empty and meaningless" are just ways of saying that life is not pre-written, that it doesn't have a pre-set meaning that we have to discover. Instead, life's meaning is something we create as we go along. As part of his awakening, Michael found that those things that used to make life seem fulfilling were really empty for him, so for a while he drifted in a vacuum without purpose or motivation, while living deeply into the question of "is life empty and meaningless, and if so, what does that mean?" Along the way, the whole topic began to lose its sting, its ability to fill him with despair. He began to say "Okay, there is this empty quality to life, but so what? Here I am, and life keeps rolling along."

And life did go on from there. Michael's black funk gradually faded to gray, then lifted significantly, enabling him to take up new endeavors that he found personally meaningful. But he had been changed in a profound way by finding himself up against something he could not change by any act of will: he developed a deep understanding of how indelible certain aspects of human conditioning can be. And as a consequence of that experience, he became far more patient with the other people in his life, knowing how difficult it can be to generate lasting changes in deep-set patterns of behavior. And, perhaps most importantly, he was able to find fundamental peace while fully in the presence of this recognition about the nature of human life.

Helpless in the face of our human limits

The truth is that there are some aspects of how you're wired that you simply *can't* change through your own efforts. What you can do is be willing to see them, and bring Presence to them. Changes, if and when they do come, happen by grace rather than by self-willed actions.

Before you are humbled to this fact, you run the risk of being heartless and even violent toward yourself and others, with an arrogant assumption that any state of being that isn't "positive" can be willed away. "Just get over it!" is a typical inner attitude to anything showing up that you don't like. The (unawakened) assumption is that the power to make these changes is in your own hands, as your personal willpower. But when you come up against something that just won't shift—that really has you by the balls and doesn't let go—then you have to bow down to what's living you, to the Source of your personal sense of self.

Great intelligence, creativity, and accomplishing power streams into life from this Source and, as you consciously surrender to it, and integrate it, you will find yourself empowered to accomplish many things. But it is a new kind of empowered, that has more to do with cooperating with the wisdom and intelligence of Being than trying to impose personal will upon it.

Core mood states

Similar to governing sentimentalities (unconscious assumptions about life), *core mood states* can be very persistent. My core mood state used to be a melancholy sadness that was gloomy and bitter-sweet. Kind of like the feeling that gets evoked by a mournful Irish ballad. It was so close to my core that I hardly ever questioned it. I even justified it: after all, life is very sad, isn't it? Think of all the hurting people, animals, even the planet itself (and me too). How else would I feel?

I was identified with this feeling-state. It felt like "me." If it happened to dissipate for a while, when it came back, like clouds gathering over the sun, I would recognize how familiar it was. Gradually, I began to notice that I felt some virtue in having this feeling, like it was part of my character. "I'm a good person because I feel things deeply and grieve for all those who are in pain." Wow! In a weird way, I *liked* feeling this deep melancholy sadness. It felt like home base, or a default setting in my wiring. And when it was gone I felt a little strange.

At a certain point I became able to just greenlight it as a part of me, no longer feeling any pressure to make it go away or to try to be more upbeat. And then, in that mysterious way things evolve when they're fully permitted, the clouds began to lift and my mood with it. More frequently I would enjoy feeling an open, clear state I began to call "neutral Presence." It's like being in life without any particular mood at all, just available for whatever life brings my way.

Core mood states come in a variety of flavors, of course. For example, a core mood state might take the form of chronic anxiety because life on earth is dangerous, or perhaps show up as frequent irritation at how unjust everything is. After all, that's how life is, right? And it's normal to feel this way, right? Yes.

Your core mood state may stem from how your particular physiology reacts to the core wound. It's not right or wrong. You might not begin noticing this "mood" until you clear some of your more dramatic reaction patterns, and spend some time quietly with yourself. It will be interesting to notice how it shows up for you. When greenlighted to be as it is, space can open up around your core mood, and you might discover that it is shifting and making room for new possibilities.

The core wound becomes conscious

At this point, you may be thinking that this integration period will bring all your shadow issues, persistent patterns, and core mood states to light and soon you will be free of them. But that's not the whole picture.

The *unconscious* core wound characteristically feels tight, or squeezing, or pressured, as if the limitations of your life are rubbing up against your intuited sense of freedom and spaciousness. When you realize that the angst at your core doesn't mean there's any-thing fundamentally wrong with you, at some point a deep relaxation occurs. It's not that the wound gets healed once and for all, but when your subconscious resistance to the wound ends, so does most of what made it so uncomfortable. For the most part, it just ceases to be a problem. Where there was tension before, now there is greater ease and wellness of Being.

At times, the juxtaposition of limits and freedom will just be what is, without feeling any particular way. But at other times, the limits will come crashing down again, with all the accompanying distress they ever brought (if not more). It seems inevitable, as long as you have a body with its pain, its aging, its grieving of losses, and its longing to fulfill its dreams, that all these things will at times bite deeply. So will the mental and emotional snarls you fall into from time to time, no matter how much shadow work you've done. Awakening does not—and cannot—take away all of your conditioning. In some ways you will still be the person you have been. Part of fully integrating your awaking is to come to terms with that, and realize it's not a bad thing.

Keep in mind that life is a dynamic process. In between plunges into broken zones, governing sentimentalities, and core mood states, the delicate new shoots of your natural, authentic self will begin emerging and growing with new vigor. Most people report that the periods of ease and flow become a greater feature of their lives in the first years after awakening, and the dark, stormy passages tend to be less frequent, or pass more quickly. But this is only a broad view: each person will encounter ups and downs in his or her own unique timing and rhythm.

Sooner or later, the pain of resisting the core wound dissipates as you become more able to feel and live a most-interesting paradoxical existence. The sense of wound gradually gives way to something that feels more like a divine Mystery—unknowable yet also somehow self-revealing, as you continue to discover the wonders and miracles of divinely human life.

This passage of integration will get easier over time. Don't give up! Persist, endure, and cooperate with the process. It's so important to keep leaning in, keep meeting with others who understand what's happening, and keep exploring the possibilities as well as the pitfalls. Periods of happiness and wellbeing will become longer, the ease of "neutral Presence" will become second nature, and trust in Being will grow ever stronger. Over time, you will more fully experience yourself as a divinely human being until one day, you won't remember what it was like to not know who you really are.

But awakening and integration is not the end of the story. You still need to get a life, and that is the topic of our final chapter.

12

Your Divinely Human Life

Our Story: As we lived forward into this new manner of experiencing life, we continued to explore the further possibilities of Awakened Heart, Awakened Mutuality, Awakened Freedom, and Awakened Purpose in company with others who were also exploring their newly-awakened potentials. Our divinely human awakening took root in us and became so unshakeable that, although we continued to weather the ups and downs of our lives, we never again lost touch with who we truly are, and our lives became imbued with the grace and ease of Being.

Things change, things stay the same

Your divinely human awakening is a passage, or a shift-point that ends one period of your life and inaugurates a new one. You begin experiencing life from a fundamentally different perspective that is no longer driven by unconscious avoidance of the core wound. And all the time and effort you once spent "seeking" is now freed up for other things. If you are like many others who have awakened to their divinely human nature, confidence in Being is growing, and the times of feeling easeful and relaxed about your life are becoming more predominant. This doesn't happen overnight, but it is a palpable trend that is typically observed in the first couple of years following the shift of the second birth.

The rest of the story is about all the ways in which you are still the same person you were before. Perhaps even more so! As the buffers that once kept you moving through life in a partially-numbed condition are removed, you may find yourself scrambling to cope with the sheer intensity of what's coming at you from all angles. And you may find yourself reacting in old, familiar ways— ways that you're not particularly happy about. But here they are.

As you've been learning (though might not have wanted to hear), embodied awakening will not automatically convey upon you supernatural powers nor will it give you a personality transplant. You're still you, paradoxically new and different and yet still, somehow, the same.

Awakening "normalizes"

After a while, you might start forgetting how it used to be before you awakened to your true nature. Being divinely human is so natural that, once you integrate it, it is difficult to imagine how anyone can *not* see how they are this remarkable blend of infinite and finite, spirit and matter. We are hard-wired to "normalize" all our experiences, even this one. What that means is that what once stood out as new and different because it was in contrast to the base state at the time becomes just part of the landscape after a while. It is no longer drawing your attention in the same way.

Further awakenings

You may remember that in Chapter 9 I discussed the three primary aspects of your Conscious nature—Awareness, Being, and Heart—and how most people awaken through one, or at most two, of these aspects. Any one of these three can reveal to you the unlimited, ever-present, unchanging nature that is the divine part of who you are, and bring with it a radically different manner of self-knowing and experiencing life.

Some people will have their seeking completely satisfied with this initial level of awakening to their divinely human nature.

Which is fine. However, others may find themselves still restless and wondering if there's something *more*. Perhaps someone who awakened through Awareness is wondering why they aren't experiencing more unconditional love, or someone who awakened through the life-current of Being still feels confused about what's meant by "witnessing." If that's the case for you, you may wish to cultivate—through meditation or other practices as described in Chapter 9—the other aspects, the ones that perhaps aren't as easy for you to "get." And even the aspect through which you did awaken may yet have more to reveal: you may have touched in with it sufficiently to awaken, but not yet explored it to the fullness of what's possible.

There is a paradox here that's useful to keep in mind. Your experience of the core wound might leave you feeling like you're "not enough" or "not good enough" or "insufficient"—because you intuit that there is an unlimited aspect to who you are that you're not able to fully embody. You automatically compare your current situation with a more idealized one, just because you have the capacity to do so. So the sense of "this awakening is not enough" *might* just be an echo from the core wound, a habitual way of relating to life as not good enough yet, or with a sense of always wanting *more*. Or maybe it's the momentum of seeking that hasn't fully unwound itself yet. So if you are questioning whether you need to awaken further, take a little time to sense into what's behind it. Is it being driven by a restless, almost habitual downplaying of *what is*, or does it come from a deeply felt prompt from your innermost Being to go further?

Development in the divinely human life typically includes a dynamic tension between stretching into new areas and landing exactly in your life as it is right now and relaxing there. It also includes getting to know who you are now, admitting your limitations to yourself and others, and then finding ways for your potentials to come forth and shine.

First you awaken, then you need to get a life

During the integration period, you'll have made many discoveries about yourself as you noticed how you were showing up, or felt new impulses inspiring you to action. Perhaps you now find yourself looking for a way to make a meaningful contribution to the world, or a way to give back to those who helped you realize your dream of awakening. Perhaps you've been focused on awakening and little else for a while now. You may wonder how to transfer your interest in awakening into useful activity in the world. You might have an intuition, or even a passion, for becoming a spiritual teacher yourself.

If so, welcome. Spiritual teaching, or other ways of supporting people in self-discovery, can be a very rewarding life-path on the heart level, if not always on the financial level. And while it seems that the number of people who are interested in embodied awakening is currently modest, there is also evidence that it's growing. The time is ripe for spiritual transformations to flourish, and there is an ever-growing need for people who can help others navigate the perilous darkness before dawn in order to arrive at a permanent awakening.

If you are so drawn, or even if you think you *might* have some interest in this area, you will want to do some preparatory work to deepen your ability to *be with* others in all the different ways they might show up. The Institute of Awakened Mutuality (IAM) offers advanced-level courses to help people integrate their awakenings, deepen in mutuality, and prepare to become mentors and teachers of Waking Down in Mutuality. You can learn more at **awakenedmutuality.org.**

Within the WDM framework, people who have awakened and have an impulse to be of service to others begin with *mentoring.* You may remember from Chapter 7 that mentors are volunteers who offer their time to listen to and support others on the path, rather like an older brother or sister. Mentoring can be a first step toward becoming a teacher of WDM, or it can be done just for its own sake. It is a low-pressure activity that can help you discover whether you have an aptitude for the type of deep listening and holding that is at the heart of WDM.

Mentoring is a gift to the one receiving it, and also brings gifts to the person doing the mentoring. There is something almost magical about the shift that occurs when you have the intention of being present for someone else. During the integration phase, or shakedown, it's easy to get swamped by the roller-coaster of emotional storms and broken zones, but when you show up for someone else who needs your care and attention, a balancing effect occurs. You are tangibly reminded that you are still making a contribution even when most of your energy is turned inward toward your own process. Plus, it's a great way to learn more about the give-and-take of mutuality in action.

So, mentoring is a valuable post-second birth activity, whether or not you go on to become a teacher of WDM. You will increase your capacity to "hold" another—to be with them without trying to fix or change them—much like the way you are learning to be with yourself from Presence as you practice Inseeing. And that greater capacity will enhance all the other relationships you might have in your life.

Other avenues of creative expression

Of course, mentoring or teaching WDM is only one of an infinite array of possibilities for expressing divinely human creativity. You might continue with whatever line of work or personal endeavor you've already been engaged in, or you might find yourself seeking something new, something more relevant to who you are now.

Whether or not you ever speak directly about your experience of awakening to your relatives or the folks you work with, you will be transmitting that awakening effortlessly, 24/7. Your very presence will be catalytic to those who are receptive to that transmission. You may not see the results directly, but you will have a positive influence and, over time, you may notice that people around you just instinctively feel more open, or more trusting, or in some other way demonstrate an increased ability to be present in their own lives and with you. Of course, your ability to be a trustworthy friend will increase gradually, as you integrate your awakening and work through some of the rougher edges of your personality. This takes some time.

Some people find themselves almost bursting with the impulse to tell others about their awakening, but if this is you, please have a care. Especially at first, you may want to hold back a bit and let the awakening mature in you a while. Then, when you do speak, you will want to stay attuned to the listener's capacity and interest in hearing what you have to share. You will be more successful if you stay sensitive to their frameworks and, where possible, use language they can understand. You may feel frustrated if you discover that most of the people around you are less than enthusiastically interested in what has been a primary focus of your life. However, it does little good to proselytize—most people have a strong radar for that kind of approach, and avoid it.

This is where creativity comes in. Perhaps there are other ways to share your new-found confidence in Being. Perhaps you will take it into music, or art, or you might find yourself moving into some form of therapy or healing work. Still others find that they can simply be a good listener to their friends—something that is still all-too-rare in our world.

In the meantime, find other people to share with who are keen to hear about your experience. Teachers, mentors, peers, your local sitting or mutuality groups—these are all good places to start. And there are WD-related events offered throughout the year which can be a great place to share experiences and make new friends.

Four areas for deepening your divinely human experience

Beyond the work of integrating your awakening through revisiting your shadow areas and broken zones in order to free up more energy and attention, you can undertake further development that will really bring your awakening into full flowering so that it becomes a dynamic force not only for your life, but for transforming the world around you as well. Here are four areas worthy of special consideration.

Awakened Heart: longing for the divine

Any awakening will touch your heart, but there is a difference between a heart that has been moved by the shifts of awakening and a fully Awakened Heart.

The divinely human Heart is remarkable in its multi-dimensionality. We experience love in so many different flavors: a child's love for his or her parents, parents' love for their children, love that draws adults together to form life partnerships, love for friends and colleagues, love of work, recreation, or creative endeavors, and so on. There is a range, or scale, of love as well. We can love fervently, fondly, deeply, unconditionally, warmly, barely, or not at all. Or even positively *not* love—as in feeling animosity or hatred. Our hearts are exquisitely sensitive parts of us, and they register not only how much or little we feel love for other people or things, they also register how much love—or lack of love—is coming toward us from others. And not only register; our hearts record and remember the things that hurt us. They may build up psycho-emotional scar tissue, or put up walls, or pad themselves as if with Styrofoam in an effort to avoid more pain. Yet still they long for, and try to, love others.

Beyond the love that is exchanged between people, there is another type of love that you might intuitively seek, and that is the pure, refined, sweet bliss of divine love, love of a Beloved that can transport you beyond your usual human cares, and beyond the fickleness that characterizes much of human love. Whether you personify the Source of that love as a divine being, or hold it as more abstract, you may long to bathe in a truly unconditional love, a love that affirms all that is good and true in you and in this manifest world. And not only to bathe in it, but to feel your own heart blown wide open, to feel the rush of that heart-love flowing outward to caress the world and each being in it. If you can imagine how it would feel to love this freely, this wildly, this unconditionally—and if you have ever had glimpses of that—you will naturally want more of it.

Or perhaps you long for a sense of your inherent perfection, or unity, or strength, truth, wisdom—whatever holy idea that appears to be missing from your experience. If your early life failed to include one or more of these core values, your energetic heart would have thickened in that region, so to speak, and you will have formed personality traits to attempt to compensate. You will be driven to seek that which you think you lack.

Awakening does not automatically heal all the wounds of your tender heart, nor does it necessarily bring you all the qualities you have been seeking. It's an ongoing process. Some of the insulation around your heart may have melted, but more self-exploration may be needed to address the deeper wounds and residue of trauma. If you feel disappointed, if your life doesn't have as much bliss and joy as you had hoped, it's probably because your heart is still defended, still partially closed.

There's nothing wrong with a defended heart, of course. The aperture of a healthy heart opens when it feels safe enough, and naturally closes part-way whenever it is in a more harsh or insensitive space. Being closed is only a problem when it is a stuck condition: when your heart simply cannot trust enough to ever open. That's a sorry way to live. It's important to remember that opening your heart usually requires persistence, sensitivity, and some help from skillful assistants.

This may be a good time to begin, or to revisit, meditating or other means of connecting with your inner divinity. You may find yourself spontaneously feeling an impulse to express devotional feelings, either to a particular avatar or deity that has meaning for you, or even toward other people who shine for you as the living embodiment of the divine. As long as devotional expressions occur between consenting adults, this can be a most beautiful, heart-opening and life-affirming practice.

Devotion isn't for everyone, however. Each body has its own manner of finding connection with that sense of transcendence, wonder, and bliss that we call *divine*. Take the time to nurture your impulses in this area, and discover what's possible for you.

As your heart is restored to its natural permeability, as it comes more fully alive, you may find yourself at times dropping into profound states. Your awakened heart naturally attunes to the highest, most refined frequencies that can be experienced. More than that, even. Beyond what can be "experienced" in the usual sense is the direct apperception of the Absolute, that which cannot be described because it is not in form. For myself, the quest was not complete until I was graced by the "non-experience" of being immersed in Source, of going *home* where all distinctions, all concerns, and the last vestiges of separation dissolved into just That. And even though experiencing returned after a while, and functional separations were once again in place, something in me just *knew* beyond any doubt that I was That and That was me, and that all was, mysteriously, right with the world. If you are called to take your experience to the edge and beyond, I feel confident that grace will smile upon you also.

Awakened Mutuality: relationships coming alive

Throughout the process of becoming divinely human, you've been learning about mutuality, which is the art of being fully and authentically expressed, while making room for others to also be fully and authentically expressed as well.

As you practice Inseeing with the many interior aspects of yourself, you are, in effect, inviting them to be in mutuality. From Presence, you are able to meet them with interested curiosity and invite them to communicate—to be fully expressed. Even triggered, reactive aspects that appear to be quite oppositional at first, when held by Presence, in time become able to coexist without stress, and without preventing life's forward movement.

The same fundamental dynamic is possible between people, when Presence, or Being, is holding the encounter and making room for the participants to fully express whatever is up for them—even when triggered. The challenge comes when the players are merged (identified) with their reactivity and unable to maintain a degree of Presence. Then issues tend to become volatile or explosive, feelings get hurt, and conflicts can appear irresolvable. Being human, this is not uncommon, and, though painful at times, isn't a sign that you're doing anything wrong.

In Chapter 8 you learned many keys to mutuality, including ways to build trust and ways to make amends when things have blown up and gotten messy. You can practice mutuality no matter where you are in your process of divinely human awakening. However, once that fundamental recognition of your true nature has occurred, another degree of mutuality becomes possible.

For one thing, you will have *more* of you available more of the time (except when you are in the throes of a shakedown passage). You will become better able to hold your own while holding others in your awareness at the same time. You will also tend to be more understanding of the challenges each person faces on account of conditioned tendencies that flare up in them without warning—those patterns that at times seem so intractable.

More than that, however, is the fundamental recognition that the person sitting across from you isn't fundamentally separate or *other.* Whether or not they have had any conscious recognition of this existential truth, you now know it. And in knowing it, you will begin to see that you cannot harm that one without, in some manner, also harming yourself. This "other realization" takes mutuality to a whole new level.

Your awakening will almost certainly bring with it a greater sense of empathy, so that you actually feel what others feel. Assuming this is the case, you will very quickly get how hurting someone near to you can bring instant pain into your own awareness. But even if you don't have this type of visceral experience, simply knowing your inherent Onlyness will make you mindful that you don't exist in a vacuum, and that your wellbeing is, to a degree, dependent on others' wellbeing. You can't have one without the other.

However, it isn't sufficient—or even appropriate—to just "be nice to everyone." The other side of the equation is that you are here as a powerful, creative being and naturally feel impelled to make your mark in the world, to be fully and authentically expressed. This impulse only grows stronger with awakening, because the more you arrive here in embodiment, the more you want to actively participate in the dance of life. So that's the challenge of awakened mutuality: being more yourself and more non-separate, both. You know you're not intrinsically separate and cannot afford to treat others poorly, yet you also know that, in order to get in the room, you have to speak what's true for you. Sometimes this might trigger pain in other bodies, even when that's not your intention. Ah, the rub!

The payoff, however, for hanging in with these kinds of difficulties and challenges, is that your relationships can take on whole new depths of intimacy as well as autonomy. As you become freer to act from your inner sense of rightness, you also begin to trust that you can make room for others to do that, too. You trust that it will all work out, even if you aren't in complete control or haven't foreseen all the possible downsides. Relationships can become sweeter, and more playful. There can be so much joy in simply being, with others who are doing the same. And gazing—that most intimate meeting, eyes to eyes, beyond words—becomes richer and deeper than ever before.

Awakened partnerships can also reach new depths of intimacy and autonomy. They will have their own unique dynamics and challenges, enough to fill another book or two. For now I will simply say that all of the inner skills of Inseeing, and the outer skills of mutuality, can be brought into your intimate relationships (with parents and children as well as lovers) to great effect. But when you live closely with another person, all your best intentions sometimes can (and will!) fly out the window at a moment's provocation. When both parties get mutually triggered, it can be nearly impossible to hear or hold the other from Presence.

So anyone who wishes to have a healthy relationship, given how complex we are as awakening beings, would do well to have a good support system, not only for themselves personally, but also for their relationship. Ideally you would have some same-gender friends who are able to listen deeply to you when you need a sounding board, in addition to whatever support you have from your divinely human teachers, mentors, Inseeing guides, and others. If you don't have others to turn to, you may put too much pressure on your intimate partner to provide everything you want and need, and that's just not going to happen all the time. Since no one can meet all the needs of another being, that's where a circle of friends can make a world of difference to the quality of your life, as well as to the health of your intimate relationships.

Some people, upon awakening, pull back from the give-and-take of human relationships and, literally or figuratively, retreat to a cave in the Himalayas to spend their time in solo contemplation. Others choose to remain engaged in the world and in relationship. The latter are more likely to find that they simply cannot stay away from mutuality. Awakened relating is the edge where Being really gets to encounter Being and find out what's possible in that interface. We are just scratching the surface of what it means to be divinely human together, and if you feel drawn to explore with those of us who are walking this path, you will be most welcome here.

Awakened Freedom

Agency refers to the capacity of individuals to act independently and to make free choices. Before exploring the awakened purpose of your life, you might want to spend a moment reflecting on the different attitudes people can have about agency. You may recall that I described four stages of embodied awakening in Chapter 1. People in Stage 1 often feel like they are *victims*, wherein other people, situations, their past, their genetic makeup, etc., are at fault for causing their pain.

People in Stage 2 of embodied awakening typically feel themselves to be *empowered creators*, believing that they can choose how they want their lives to be. They feel like powerful individuals with freedom to pursue their wants and desires. However, what they choose to create at this stage may be more about avoiding the pain of the core wound than a genuine expression of spontaneous creativity.

People in Stage 3 are beginning to realize the limits of their power to create or control their lives. There are some elements that are simply beyond anyone's power to control, including the existential fact of a core wound as well as the complex inter-weaving of forces that make up the world and social milieu. With this realization comes *surrendering* to the apparent limits in which we find ourselves immersed. Realizing you are an integral part of a vast, mysterious creation brings the attendant relief that comes when you realize you're not personally responsible for a system that is fundamentally beyond your control.

You can see how the human story is interwoven with the question of agency. Who or what is making *all this* happen? Is the locus of control within the individual, or is it in some ineffable divine Being or impersonal Universe? These are weighty questions that philosophers and spiritual realizers have debated at length. If you believe you are the doer, you will feel empowered to create your life as you choose, yet you may also blame yourself for limits and shortcomings. If you believe "God" is the doer, you may be relieved of some guilt, but feel helpless to change anything.

When you awaken to Onlyness—when you know beyond concepts that you are inherently both human *and* divine—it is natural to revisit the question, "Where is the locus of action and control over my life?" If you are both the doer and not the doer, from what source does any action arise?

First, it will be useful to remember that many, if not most, of your actions are basically automatic. They are repetitions of conditioned responses and reactions to stimuli—patterned behavior that is automatically repeated whenever particular situations present themselves. Even what you "freely choose" may be determined in large part by the conditioned filters through which you perceive.

However, there is another factor that comes into play as you are more able to be in Presence with all the conditioned parts of yourself. When you use Inseeing to bring conscious Presence to all the elements of a situation (the felt senses), and are neither merging with nor exiling any of those elements, then something new can emerge, spontaneously, out of Being. Eugene Gendlin, the father of Focusing, calls this mystery the "implicit"—the place from which something potential or implied emerges into form.

Call it implicit, or emergent, or the *now*, this is the heart of genuine, spontaneous creativity. Most of us long to bring forth what is real in us, that which is most authentic, or most lovely. Or most heart-felt. And that arises out of the Mystery, when we are in Presence with all our conditioning yet acting freely rather than automatically re-acting.

Awakened Freedom calls for a deep contemplation of the ways we are free yet bound, the doer yet not the doer. You do not need to blame yourself for how things are. You did not, and cannot, control the outcomes of any action you might take, not to mention the actions of other people. But Awakened Freedom does not mean irresponsibility or passive resignation. It is the art of being as fully informed as possible in any given moment, and then allowing actions to spontaneously emerge. You honor your divinely human life by acting *as if* you have personal power, while bowing down to the Mystery that is living in you, as you, and as the world.

Awakened Purpose

The key to awakened action is *enjoyment*. Enjoyment (or the more intense feeling of enthusiasm) is the felt sense that occurs when you are linked into the universal creative power itself. As you envision your life's purpose, you can use enjoyment as a touchstone, a way to get feedback about any endeavor you might undertake. Of course, when you attempt anything that is challenging there will be times of difficulty and frustration, but you can check to see if the overall activity is enjoyable for you. Remember those sensual delights you were encouraged to play with along the way to awakening? That was to help you open your channels of enjoyment. If an activity is not exactly enjoyable (like some of the chores life requires), is it at least acceptable? If it isn't, if you find yourself continually disliking or resenting the activity, you are going against the natural flow of Being in your life, and may do yourself or others harm in the process.

Some divinely human people, upon coming into their awakening, expect their true life purpose to show up in some sort of a grand display. They are waiting for a sign—a powerful dream vision, or some remarkable synchronicity—something that would feel so compelling there would be no doubt, no hesitation about dedicating their life to that divine Purpose or calling.

And perhaps it will come to you in just that manner. Or more subtly. Or you might simply have more options to choose from than One Big One. If your purpose is not blatantly obvious to you, you might try noticing where your interests take you. Go to a bookstore and notice the sections you gravitate toward. Or notice the people you are drawn to spend time with, and what topics engage you. In many cases, your destiny will somehow reveal itself out of your interpersonal relationships.

If in doubt, you might try serving others, or volunteering to help support the spiritual work or works that were most helpful in your awakening process. Embodied awakening is a *yin* process, mostly. Even when practiced in mutuality, it requires a strong inward focus that often leaves little energy for outward activity in the world. As you deepen in and integrate that awakening, you will find your *yang* energy for active engagement gradually returning. There is no need to rush this process; it will take time. But, at some point the need for your awakening to find expression will become stronger, and you will want to heed that. Otherwise, if the awakening doesn't find its voice, if it is not expressed, a sickness of the soul, or depression, can arise.

If it's been a long hard road

If you are having a difficult time getting your life back into motion, you might still be depleted from the stress of the awakening process itself. Not everyone has a particularly difficult journey into awakening, so if that's true for you, terrific! But if you had to go through a lot, if your dark night included many losses, or if your shakedown has been particularly harrowing, now is the time to acknowledge and honor how hard it's been to get here. Mixed in with the joy of discovering new capacities, you may—understandably—be feeling some resentment at God or Being or the divine One that sometimes felt absent or unreliable, that didn't keep you as safe as you wanted to be. Or there may be layers of grieving for what has been endured. Please be especially tender and gentle with yourself, and frequently stop and acknowledge the path itself, and your courage for traveling it. You've done well!

You may also find yourself, with your heart more open than ever, feeling sadness for the others in the world who have not yet been able to get here fully. Again, take whatever time you need to feel the rich array of emotions that have been stirred by the profound process you've undergone. And when you are ready, give it all your blessing and step boldly forward into your new life.

Celebrating your awakened life

One day you'll emerge from the more intense period of integration and discover a sense of ease, or wellness, bubbling up on its own accord. Allow yourself to celebrate arriving here in the wholeness and joy of awakened life.

You may find once again a sense of bliss, or feel a deeper connection to Source or Being, a connection that might have felt absent for a while during the more challenging encounters with your shadow zones. Perhaps it feels like the sun is returning after a long gray period of darkness and rain. Or perhaps it feels like your inner sun is shining now—for the first time ever in your life.

For some people, new sensitivities or abilities may begin appearing. Perhaps it takes the form of being more empathic with others, or perhaps some psychic abilities are becoming available for you now. Quite a few people find a deep sense of resonance with nature and feel drawn toward a ritual, or shamanic, path that helps them engage with that world. Still others find their hearts moved by devotional singing, ecstatic dancing, or sitting with heart-centered teachers who inspire them to deeper experiences of divine bliss.

Many find themselves fundamentally content to simply live and be as they are moved in each moment. There is so much variety in people that it would be pointless to generalize or create an expectation for how *your* awakened life is going to look and feel. Except for this: you will find that ease of Being and trust in Being grow stronger over time.

Equilibrium

Sometimes your life will flow easily, and sometimes you'll be plunged, yet again, into some triggered reactive state where it feels like all your progress is gone in a flash. "Ugh, I'm here again." What I've found is that, while some of my broken zones appear to have been fully "healed" so that they do not throw me like they used to, I can still get triggered. Over time, it happens less frequently and when it does, I'm more quickly able to notice and bring Presence to the triggered parts. The net effect is that, more of the time, I am in a state of openness and availability to what life is bringing. But I don't expect to feel good all the time—

because I'm embodied and bodies are always cycling through the whole gamut of feeling states.

It's helpful to remember that most people do not automatically recognize "good enough." It's true! There is an inbuilt driver that keeps restlessly searching out perceived flaws and imperfections, even when our lives are fundamentally safe and sufficient. Even those who have made peace with the core wound of existence may still find a nagging sense of "not good enough" showing up. When this happens, question it. Take a moment to pull back and take a bigger view of your life. Are you safe enough? Is there a roof over your head, and are there clothes on your back? Is your partner a decent, kind person? Does your work provide enough resources to meet your basic needs? Your life may not be perfect, or it may not be ideal in this moment, but always seeking "a better life" can leave you out of balance. If you habitually strive for something more, you may never arrive at a place of contentment with what is.

You can teach yourself to notice the ways in which your life—in which *you*—are good enough right now. You might begin with a simple exercise: each night before going to bed jot down three things about you or your life right now that are good enough. Then just send a bit of appreciation to those things. In this way you'll start to recognize "good enough" more often, which will bring more peace and less worry into your daily life.

"Good enough" is not the same as settling for. You can appreciate all the ways in which your life is sufficient, and use that as a starting place from which to undertake creative new endeavors. It doesn't mean "stop here," it just means you know you're okay right now even in the midst of all the inevitable imperfections of life. Real happiness comes from being able to hold the dynamic tensions of life—all the ways our lives (or the world) could be better, and all the ways our lives (or the world) are totally okay as they are—with a lighthearted, playful outlook that comes from standing firmly in the ground of Being, knowing that you are a precious, totally unique, and *indestructible* event of creation—even while being a tender, vulnerable, finite human person. Blessed be!

Living down

"Living down" means being awake and embodied. It means allowing life to impact you deeply, allowing yourself to be touched, moved, inspired, and at times devastated. It means not avoiding feeling what there is to feel, or numbing out, or living in some lofty transcendent state where real human feelings and reactions are reduced to a minimal level. It means having passion, and allowing yourself to be impacted, and penetrated. It doesn't, however, mean "down" in a negative way—it's more like "getting down" with life, where it moves you and shakes you. Living down is as much about passion, lust, romance, and creativity as it is about feeling difficult feelings. And although at first look it might not seem very spiritual, it is in this very "down" place that you come fully alive as the embodiment of infinite Spirit.

Remember that continuing to move through the entire range of human states is what's normal in embodied awakening. When you are up, enjoy it! When you dive, dive deeply and find out what needs your loving attention. And to whatever degree you can in the moment, lend a hand to your fellow-travelers as they ride the ups and downs of this human experience. It's so much easier when the journey is shared with like-minded others!

Further awakening: seamless Onlyness

In Chapter 1, I described a fourth stage of embodied awakening called "seamless Onlyness," where the paradoxical both/and quality of divinely human awakening finally merges into a seamlessness that no longer feels like different qualities being juxtaposed, but more like a natural wholeness of Source, subjects, objects, and experiences all flowing together in a dynamic dance that contains opposites but feels inherently unified.

This stage seems to arrive gradually. It appears that the core of the separate self-sense that persisted for awhile in tandem with the awakened Conscious nature dissolves over time, thus providing an ever-growing sense of freedom, spontaneity, and delight in living. Perhaps the "ego," upon learning that no one (or no other part of us) is trying to remove it by force, at long last puts down its porcupine quills and begins purring like a kitten.

Seamless Onlyness is when the real payoff of awakening kicks in. The bulk of the work of falling apart, coming awake, and then integrating, is behind you now. More and more you find your contact with the luminous divine to be strong and steady, your heart filled with radiating warmth, and your thoughts rather effortlessly turning to whatever work is at hand. Your questions about who you are and your purpose in life have been resolved—at least well enough to give you a good measure of peace and contentment.

Your capacity for being with *all* of life is wide, and you effortlessly transmit a sense of ease to everyone around you. As you become less concerned about yourself, you become deeply available to others, with great compassion, knowing how very difficult it is to be fully here as a conscious, loving being.

You recognize that there is nothing that is not divine. Every bit of it. All of the opposites of Consciousness and matter, infinite and finite, heaven and earth have now fused into an indivisible unity of cosmic Mystery—and you are That.

These are only words attempting to point toward something ineffable. This integral stage of embodied awakening is still new, and still being explored by the handful of people who have been fortunate enough to find themselves here. I have endeavored, in this book, to describe, primarily, the precursor to this stage, the stage of coming apart, then re-constellating as an awakened divinely human being. To arrive here in conscious embodiment is a remarkable thing. However, for all of you who've been wondering, as you read through this material, "When does it start to feel more like enlightenment?" well, this is it. The long journey *down* reaches its bottom and then, naturally and organically, again ascends, only this time nothing is left out, nothing need be excluded. We are whole and complete and able to welcome whatever life may bring.

Embodied awakening might not ever fully look like the classical enlightenment that stands apart from the travails of human life. We are pioneering something new here, something that is now possible in Being that may not have been possible before. I am so glad to have met you here as you read these pages, and hope that one day we will meet in the flesh, body to body and gaze to gaze. Then we will explore, together, what it means to *become divinely human.*

ACKNOWLEDGMENTS
AND RESOURCES

My heartfelt thanks go to everyone who has contributed to this book.

First, to Saniel Bonder who pioneered a radical new approach to spiritual awakening that honored the inherent divinity of body, mind, and emotions, as well as spirit. Teaching the "Human SUN Seminar," created by Saniel and his wife-partner Linda, in the early days of my awakened service helped hone my understanding of—and ability to communicate—this new dharma, and thus laid the foundation for this book. The website for the work of Saniel and Linda is **sanielandlinda.com**.

Next, I thank Ann Weiser Cornell and Barbara McGavin, who took the basics of Gene Gendlin's Focusing to a very refined level with their Inner Relationship Focusing—which, in turn, is the foundation of the Inseeing Process described in this book. Inner Relationship Focusing, more than any other process I have explored, dovetails perfectly with Waking Down in Mutuality. Ann's website is **focusingresources.com**.

Creating a good book is a team effort. I thank all those people without whose assistance this book would never have made it off my computer. In particular, I bow to my editor Ruthie Hutchings whose editorial midwifing and loving friendship supported me through the challenging process of turning my very rough first draft into a real book; to my coach at Mission Publishing, Kim Olver, who kept me on track and moving toward my goals; to Zoë Snyder who applied her creative brilliance to the cover artwork and interior layout; to Ellen Holmes who offered her careful reading and constructive input; and to my dear husband, Michael Radford, who skillfully gave the book its final copyediting—as well as patiently enduring my months of preoccupation with this project—while always encouraging and inspiring me along the way.

I owe deep gratitude to my students, who have been so remarkably open and vulnerably present with me—I am forever touched and enriched by knowing you. And to all my teachers along the way, too many to mention individually, I bow to you with love and appreciation. You know who you are.

I am also grateful to all the furry ones who have blessed my life in so many ways over the years. They brought me their undying Presence and their boundless Hearts, and inspired me to try to be as generous and loving as they are.

I give a nod to the Institute of Awakened Mutuality, for their dedication to spreading the core values of Waking Down in Mutuality though retreats and advanced-level courses. Their website is **awakenedmutuality.net.**

I especially honor all the precious teachers and mentors who embody the heart of Waking Down in Mutuality, and continue to push the edges of what's possible for divinely human beings. You are my "second family of origin" and your boundless love and support has made me whole. You will find the teachers and mentors listed at **wakingdown.org.**

I thank mentor Bob Valine for making many personal stories of embodied awakening available through his book, *Dancing in the Fire: Stories of Awakening in the Heart of Community.* This book is available at **amazon.com.**

I also honor, beyond my ability to express, the inner Guides who have accompanied me through this life-walk, loving and encouraging me to persevere even through the darkest times. Thank you for your assistance and guidance. I wouldn't be here without you, and I am honored to be of service.

To contact CC Leigh and for information on her offerings related to divinely human awakening and Inseeing, please visit **divinelyhuman.com.**

GAZING PHOTO

Made in the USA
Lexington, KY
19 December 2011